Go Make Disciples

EMBRACE JESUS' LAST WORDS
AS YOUR MAIN CALLING

March 22, 2017
    Happy Birthday, David — It's an
honor to work alongside you at
WacoTours. You have embraced Jesus'
calling on your life — Blessings in Jesus —
                    Melinda Seibert

DREW STEADMAN

Go Make Disciples

Published by Clear Day Publishing, a division of Clear Day Media Group LLC, Waco, TX. cleardaypublishing.com.

Published in association with Lux Creative {theluxcreative.com}

Scripture quotations are taken from The Holy Bible, New International Version®, NIV® Copyright © 1973, 1978, 1984, 2011 by Biblica, Inc.® Used by permission. All rights reserved worldwide.

ISBN: 978-0-9863734-6-6

Library of Congress Control Number: 2016958155
Cover Design: Kyle Rogers
Interior Design: Lux Creative {theluxcreative.com}
Printed in the United States of America.

Dedication

To my wife, Bethany – Thank you for your love, support, and prayers. You've spurred me on to pursue Jesus in countless ways and have been a place of encouragement as I try to live it out. I love you with all my heart.

To my children, Grace, Abby Joy, Audrey, and Joshua – The opportunity to walk with you in your discipleship journey is one of the greatest joys of my life.

To the men and women who discipled me – My parents who laid the ultimate foundation of modeling what it means to follow God, be a man, a husband, a father, and leader; My in-laws who revealed to me whole new aspects of God's heart and what it means to be a disciple; Robert Herber who pursued me when I was a flake and laid lasting foundations in my life; and Jimmy Seibert who modeled what it means to wholeheartedly follow Jesus and lead others to do the same. The words within these pages come from each of your influence.

To the pastors, Lifegroup leaders, church planters, and disciple-makers of the Antioch Movement – These are your stories. Thank you for the countless prayers, commitment, and sacrifice which is often unseen, that laid the foundation for a movement. You are my heroes and my main regret is the inability to highlight even more of your stories.

Table of Contents

Introduction

August 2001

I tentatively walked through the old, aluminum-framed doors of Antioch Community Church, faintly noticing the musty smell lingering inside the former grocery store. The small step across the threshold proved a prophetic moment. Every journey begins with a solitary step; my path of transformation was no different.

It was my first year of college, and I blissfully failed to grasp the significance of those early weeks. My concerns centered on the basic emotional needs of friendship and acceptance, not yet aware that behind the scenes God had set in motion a seismic change.

My life at this point defined an all-too-normal Christian-living paradox – though I heralded from a dynamic church and healthy family, I sought my pleasure and identity from the things of the world. My energy was dominated by the delicate balance of just enough sin to not be too much.

Hidden sin ruled my life, I rarely spent time with God, and I never shared my faith. As I reflect back on those years, I now see that my spiritual life was a mere veneer to cover the worldliness underneath. Sure, I desired God and desired His purposes, but I would have never realized His call on my life. I exemplified the ideal setup for a later spiritual crash, and I shudder to think of the consequences without the intervention of God.

The transformation began when I met a man named Robert who invited me to his new Lifegroup. This soon expanded into an invitation to a guys' discipleship group for several other freshmen men. I attended for a few months but never really participated. While others poured out their hearts and confessed their struggles, I made excuses. Truth be told, I cannot believe Robert kept pursuing me.

Time went by and, against all odds, Robert managed to trick me into attending a mission trip to Mexico over Spring Break. A few weeks after I paid the deposit, I discovered that all of my friends decided to go skiing. I was upset, but it was past the point of backing out so I begrudgingly boarded the charter bus at 5am on a crisp Saturday morning. I sat in the back, alone and perilously close to the toilet. For the next eleven hours the bathroom smells wafted over my seat as I spent the entire ride listening to music and simultaneously chastising myself for such social stupidity.

Despite my lack of faith, the trip proved dynamic. For the first time in my life, I actually fully lived out my faith. It wasn't anything new; rather, I simply applied basic practices of Kingdom living.

While on the trip, I woke up every day and connected with Jesus. I distinctly remember watching the sun rise above the stucco hotel walls, eagerly awaiting the flash of warmth to wash my body of the cold morning air as I learned to spend time with God. I watched the power of God heal people on the street during the outreaches and embraced the privilege of helping people commit their lives to Christ for the first time. The freedom from sin and worldly influence I experienced was a marked relief from my normal life. By the end of the trip, I didn't want to leave; in fact, I grieved for my friends skiing down the pristine slopes of Colorado.

The entire experience culminated on the bus ride home. I gazed out on the pitch black sky as we rumbled along Interstate 10 through the vast expanse of West Texas. Everyone was asleep on the bus except for our small group. We shared our stories late into the night until the conversation finally paused. Robert filled the silence by provocatively asking us, "So what are you going to do about it?"

Time froze for me in this holy moment. Something welled up within me, a sharp moment of clarity, causing me to blurt out, "Whatever it takes!" I tasted the life of a disciple, and I was resolved to do whatever it took to keep it.

This set me on a journey of transformation. Like any story, mine has had ups and downs, but I can honestly say that the resolve remains. Though it would be easy to infer that my life was changed by this trip to Mexico, I believe it was something else entirely.

The trip was powerful, but it was the previous months and the latter years of consistent discipleship meetings that led to lasting change. I don't remember much of what Robert said in our meetings; I've forgotten the content of most of the lessons and books I read during those years. But the *consistency of a discipleship community over time* completely transformed me and, equally important, empowered me to stay transformed.

The mission trip was a catalyst, a necessary one, but without discipleship it would dissolve to a mere footnote in my life's story, another church high gradually tapering off into the atmosphere of my worldly living.

I've now worked at Antioch Community Church for more than a decade, and part of my responsibilities include overseeing discipleship. For us, discipleship describes the journey of spiritual growth we all take into the image of Christ, and discipleship also defines the responsibility to lead others into the same. In fact, I believe the two cannot be separated. To be a disciple you must also go make disciples. At our church, we utilize curriculum and teach classes, but discipleship primarily refers to small group communities, such as the one described in my story. I wholeheartedly believe discipleship must be life-on-life and cannot be mass-produced through books or teaching. Over time, this model has born tremendous fruit. So much so that pastors of other churches occasionally hear about Antioch's discipleship and travel to Waco to learn more. There seems to be a broad awareness of the importance of rediscovering this spiritual truth across the body of Christ. I'm often given the privilege of hosting these leaders.

However, I've started to notice a trend in most of these conversations. The pastors tend to arrive eager to discover our secret sauce for discipleship. But instead, we inevitably reach a point in the conversation when it suddenly dawns on them that, at least on paper, *their* church utilizes a far better system and a more robust curriculum than we use at Antioch.

It's often an awkward moment as I notice their disappointment, especially considering they spent considerable time and money to learn from us. For a brief moment, I feel like a pastoral con man who has tricked unwitting pastors into driving to Waco and handing over their discipleship material – all without giving them anything in return.

But for some reason, our discipleship is still very effective and, despite their well-researched discipleship process, these church leaders still discern that something is still missing in their approach. After sitting through many of these meetings, I believe God has highlighted a missing piece to the discipleship equation.

I find we all tend to overlook the most critical factor: *Culture*. By the grace of God, we have a deep discipleship *culture* at Antioch. At times in our church's history we've supplemented the culture with a great process and a great curriculum, and at other times we've barely given any support at all, yet the culture remains. Cultures take a long time to create, but once created, will endure a long time.

I have good news and bad news for you. The good news is that you too can create a culture; it's actually not very complicated. The bad news is that building a culture will take many years and a painstaking commitment to not give up. No big deal.

But seriously, you can do this; students, retirees, stay-at-home moms, business leaders, teachers and pastors all make wonderful disciple-makers. Discipleship is relationships, thus there is no formula. That being said, there are many important practices which will lead you down the path of disciple-making. I pray you are empowered to take the next steps, and perhaps avoid a few pitfalls along the way.

I'm deeply thankful for my senior pastor, Jimmy Seibert and his wife Laura. Nearly fifteen years prior to my arrival, they committed to establish a discipleship culture. They started with only seven people and for the first several years, they saw very little external fruit. They endured countless obstacles – relational, spiritual, and financial, yet they continued to persevere. Gradually this discipleship culture grew until it blossomed, deeply imbedded into hundreds of lives. There was no one moment, just a lifestyle of persistence. This culture served as the foundation for planting Antioch Community Church over a decade later, and it remains the foundation upon which all of our other ministry rests.

Today, thirty years later, it's easy to see the impact – the Antioch Movement has thirty churches across the United States, in addition to more than sixty international missions teams scattered across the world. Our local church in Waco, Texas is vibrant and healthy, filled with hundreds of disciple-making Lifegroups and a widespread local outreach. But it all started with a few tenacious people who committed to make disciples and who refused to give up.

Jesus described the Kingdom of Heaven as a mustard seed in an oft-overlooked, short parable found in Matthew 13:31-32. It's compared to the tiniest of seeds but contains the promise of growing into the largest garden tree. Consider His words as a blueprint for making disciples: a discipleship culture will almost always start small but if the DNA is right, over time it will grow into a transformational force. Internally, I often wrestle with this hard truth. I'd much rather preach or lead a ministry or do something (really anything) exciting than take the time to patiently invest in a few other men. I can easily deceive myself into believing my calling is to transplant plants rather than to plant seeds. But the Kingdom doesn't work this way according to both the words and the model of Jesus.

I'm grateful for the example of the Seiberts, alongside the many others who prioritized discipleship over other more exciting ministry opportunities. Jimmy still preached, traveled, and administrated, but first he discipled – in fact, in the early years of Antioch he met with sixteen men in one-on-one discipleship relationships. Years later I reaped the benefit, and I'm committed that years from now the people who walk through our church doors will experience the same.

Whether you are discipling one person, leading a Lifegroup, or pastoring a church, don't worry about the size of your group; instead focus on setting the right DNA, even if it's just one person. It will take time, but if you don't give up then thirty years from now, you too will witness incredible stories of transformation.

Discipleship is a missing ingredient in the body of Christ, and I believe God is re-awakening us to the importance of this basic, yet powerful spiritual practice. I pray the following pages both inspire you and empower you to *Go Make Disciples*.

CHAPTER 1

Why Discipleship?

Jason slowly loaded a shell into the twelve-gauge shotgun lying across his lap. The newly chambered round clicked into place, an ominous portend interrupting the tense silence. Sweat dripped down his face and shaking hands gripped the handle as he stared ahead to the end of his life. In this hopeless moment, he contemplated how dramatically his life had unraveled. He once dreamed of raising a family and living productively but this fading image appeared now as a mere mirage. His physical body reflected his life; once strong, drugs reduced his frame to a mere 135 pounds. Jason was literally wasting away.

Meth had ravaged his body for longer than he could remember. For many years he thought he was able to manage his addiction. He sold drugs for a living and then split the proceeds to feed his habit and provide for his family. He lived with Monica, his long-time girlfriend, and their kids. Together their life was a tenuous balance of seeking to parent their children while still holding on to their lifestyle. This worked for a while, but sin and drugs are cruel masters, demanding full control. Something had to give.

Monica recognized the slow creeping destruction and bravely announced she was done with drugs. Jason listened patiently, while simultaneously refilling his pipe to take his next hit. "Sure," he replied half-heartedly, but with no intention of stopping himself. Her attempts produced some change in her own life; his reluctance pushed him further down the path of addiction.

Life continued a façade of normality for a few months, until the day Jason returned home to a half-empty house. Assuming a robbery, he ran through the ransacked rooms to gauge the situation and plot his next steps. In the course of preparation, he remembered his obligation to call Monica to check in and inform her of the crime. He held the phone, bracing for her to respond with the disbelief and anger of a typical robbery victim, but was mildly shocked by her strange calmness. Their brief call flipped his world upside down when he learned he completely misread the situation. No one stole anything – she left him, and took the kids with her. Jason was now alone.

His self-destruction escalated after Monica's surprising choice to leave the home. Hope faded, building to this crisis moment cradling his gun while in a drug-altered state preparing to end his life.

Pause. His story should end right here. Drug addiction, broken relationships, generations of family dysfunction, and a pervasive sinful culture build a powerful bulwark to change which stymies even the best teachers and social scientists. We've stared this problem in the face for decades and are no closer to a solution. Jason should be another statistic.

Jason sat for a long moment, and then popped the shotgun shell out, not quite ready to end it all. But as soon as he set down the gun, a new wave of hopelessness hit and he reloaded, only to back down once more. This struggle continued all night long. The immediate crisis finally passed, but with no lasting resolution. Days went by, then months, and destruction still appeared inevitable, a mere question of timing.

Jason eventually reached a new breaking point. But this time, he miraculously reached for his pen instead of his gun. He had seldom attended a church and did not have any relationship with Christ but somehow knew God was his only hope. He wrote God a letter to express his deep need. His pent up frustration was like a dam threatening to burst as the initial confession cracked the walls trapping him. The trickle turned into a stream and the stream gave way to torrent. His pain poured out on the pages, and with it his anguish budded into a fledgling resolve.

After writing he stood up, walked straight to his room, grabbed his drugs and flushed them down the toilet. Whatever determination he lacked to end his life he discovered in order to save it.

It's a powerful story, yet profoundly incomplete. These dramatic moments fit a pervasive, but false, motif. We long to see stories of brokenness, like Jason's, experience a Cinderella transformation of sudden change. We want to see the narrative instantly change into a story of redemption, a story that ends "happily ever after," but life never works this way. If Jason's story ended here, with this moment of resolve, we'd soon discover that the moment was simply that: a moment. His destruction would have been delayed, not averted. Jason needed much more.

God faithfully responded to the letter … in the form of handcuffs. Shortly after this experience, Jason was pulled over and arrested for possession of drugs. The police missed the large stash hidden in his car, but still found enough to take him to jail. He initially determined to fight the charges, only to learn the DEA knew all about his activities. A prison sentence was just a matter of time.

He initially received probation, only to promptly fail a drug test and return to the police station. Jason defiantly stood up to leave while his probation officer outlined the new charges, but as he turned away, the Lord interrupted him and spoke clearly to His heart, "You asked for my help. Here it is." He paused for a long moment as he stood before this new fork in the road. Jason sighed, sat back down, and accepted the plea deal for a year in state prison; he recognized jail as an invitation from God, an intervention to set him free.

While incarcerated, Jason joined a Bible study and Christian community behind bars. He had no access to drugs, which broke his addiction. As a result, his body slowly rebuilt its physical strength. Likewise, his spiritual strength grew as he studied the Bible. The time was not without pain; he never once heard from Monica or his family, but the seeds of change were taking root.

Nearly one year after he walked into the jail, he stepped out again, this time a free man – both physically and spiritually. But unknown to him, these first few days of freedom were perhaps the most significant of all. Many others had stood in his same shoes, finding God in jail, resolving to change, and then finding themselves back in addiction when they could not break free from the shackles of their broken life. Shockingly high recidivism rates mark prisons across our nation, all the more so when the former inmate lacks a healthy support structure and has a history of drug abuse. Change had already begun in Jason, but the coming weeks would determine its full effect.

When Jason returned home to Waco, Texas, he spent the first night on a relative's couch. As he lay down, he noticed the bedroom light on underneath the door as the occupants smoked drugs all night long. The moving shadows danced beneath the doorframe, a siren song inviting him back. While he resolved to change, the odds remained stacked against him.

Jason knew he needed Christian community to survive but didn't know where to find it. In fact, all he knew was the name of a church called Antioch. Two years earlier, Jason took his son trick-or-treating while high on meth and a man approached him to share the Gospel. Jason didn't accept Jesus but did receive prayer. The man enthusiastically invited him to church and Jason agreed to go, primarily to end the conversation. He never went, but years later, it was still the one church he knew.

Jason had no idea how he'd be received or what to expect that first Sunday. He wandered through the doors with his son into a crowded lobby. He stood alone, a bit overwhelmed at what to do next, when a woman approached him and introduced herself as Amy. She saw his discomfort and invited him to sit next to her family. As they sat down, Jason briefly met her husband Jim and the service began. He enjoyed the church service, but did not experience a dramatic display of spiritual power or receive a life-altering prophetic word. To an outside observer, the whole experience would appear deceptively normal, even boring.

Afterward, Jim struck up a conversation and they talked for a while as Amy picked up the kids. Their conversation reached a natural end, but as Jim turned to leave, he took a step, oddly paused and then turned around and invited Jason to lunch with his family.

Thirty minutes later as the children greedily consumed pizza before scampering off to play, the adults eventually found space to discuss the challenges of Jason's life, despite the natural interruptions of an occasional child's request. After the meal, Jim took another step and invited Jason to Lifegroup that evening.

The first group meeting was an interesting cultural contrast. They picked Jason up from his inner city home, drove to the other side of town, and together stepped inside the large suburban house. The room was filled with successful businessmen and women, most of whom were long-time believers. He initially felt distinctly out-of-place, but was warmly greeted before the thought had a chance to take root.

He later recollected that, despite his differences, he never once felt like a project or an outsider at Lifegroup. He was entirely unlike these people, yet was still entirely welcomed. They treated him as a friend and that simple, authentic discipleship community transformed his life. And the impact did not stop with him.

During this time, he sought to mend his relationship with Monica. He arrived unannounced on her doorstep for the first time in over a year and, as she answered, she was taken aback by the man standing in front of her. Jason looked completely different. He appeared strong and healthy, even his speech had changed. But the years of pain produced natural skepticism – was he real? Was such a change possible? Gradually, God restored their relationship. They rebuilt friendship and trust, which led to renewed love for one another. However, old habits die hard. Their past culture did not value marriage and all they knew was a worldly perspective of romance. Monica quickly became pregnant and, for the first time in his life, Jason felt conviction regarding marriage and sexual purity.

He repented to Monica and to his Lifegroup and sought counsel in order to pursue a righteous relationship. Jim began to meet consistently with Jason for discipleship and Amy met with Monica. Jason eventually proposed and the couple vowed to remain pure until their marriage.

More than anything else, Jason considers the impact of discipleship community to be the greatest catalyst for this change. Yes, he experienced dynamic decision points, but it was the consistency of community that provided the lasting foundation for change. The transformation extended to every aspect of his life. It changed his parenting and marriage, and he finally found steady employment.

As part of his own discipleship process, Jason began reaching out to others. He diligently prayed for his boss and began to build a friendship. The two men ate lunch together weekly for several months; the man was impressed by the reality of Jason's new life yet showed no interest in Christ or in church. Though he steadfastly refused to attend a service, he did agree to attend Jason's wedding.

The ceremony was a powerful display of redemption; it was church in the fullest sense of the word. The next morning, Jason's boss looked over at his own wife, and together they decided to attend church for the first time in many years. That Sunday, they both received Christ. Over time, each of their children accepted Christ as did several other family members. The former skeptic is now a Lifegroup leader.

Jason's family also experienced a dynamic change. His brother, mother, and sister all received Jesus, along with many other relatives. All told, at least fifteen of Jason's extended family members have turned to the Lord.

Others noticed the change and started to ask questions. Jason was previously well known on the streets and connected to multiple gangs; his former colleagues initially viewed his new life with skepticism, but as the change endured, they started to seek his help. Many ex-gang members committed their lives to the Lord, so much so that I jokingly think we have enough gang veterans to run our city. But seriously, we do.

I estimate several hundred people – almost all from the inner city of Waco – have turned to Jesus and connected to Antioch as a result of Jason. His influence eventually reached the ears of civic leaders. He embodied something society desperately longs for yet seldom witnesses – a transformed life, a former criminal, a former addict, a former prisoner metamorphosing into a productive and healthy member of society.

Years later, Jason's testimony was portrayed on the front page of the local newspaper, the Waco Tribune-Herald. His story was upheld as a shining example of hope for ex-cons. The police chief publically declared that he once thought such stories impossible. Jason became a beacon of hope – for both city officials and for gang members. This is the power of church. This is the power of discipleship. And our world desperately longs for it.

Jason's story is powerful. And yet one of the most critical moments was the simplicity of a family Lifegroup leader introducing themselves at church and inviting him to lunch. No clouds parted, no trumpet sounded from Heaven. The kids still misbehaved at the table. The adult conversation was still interrupted by little voices. But this holy moment changed the trajectory of hundreds of lives.

Jason's enduring testimony was made possible through mundane discipleship. In reflecting on his past, he paused for a long moment before sharing, "I don't know what would have happened to me if it weren't for Jim and Amy." Never forget that simple, boring things change the world.

You may never serve on a civic committee or appear on the front page of the paper, but you can say "hi" to someone, you can invite someone to your small group, and you can commit to helping others build foundations through discipleship. It may feel tedious, and it might not always seem to make an immediate impact, but it will change the world.

Your contribution matters. Discipleship is often quite ordinary, boring even, yet if we commit to consistently live out the basics of our faith, then we too will turn around and see a legacy in our wake. Whether you are a stay-at-home mom, a teacher, a student, a business person, or in between jobs, you play a significant role.

Discipleship is critically important for spiritual growth. This simple process lays the basic foundations of faith, without which nothing else stands. And *you* can do it.

FOUNDATIONS

Bonanno Pisano designed his most famous landmark nearly a thousand years ago. Today, people still easily recall his ornate vision, which stands as a wonderful example of medieval Romanesque style. A proud Italian seaport commissioned Pisano to expand its cathedral, viewing it as a matter of civic pride. The architect used the opportunity to demonstrate his advanced knowledge of arches and load distribution, technology far ahead of its time. The designer was brilliant, the town was expanding, the blueprint was groundbreaking.

Unfortunately, none of it matters. The reason for Pisano's global fame is his glaring failure. His beautiful design focused on external beauty … and it completely neglected the foundation. The Leaning Tower of Pisa endures as a monument to poor planning, more a memorial to the danger of a quick fix than a breakthrough in Italian architecture.

The ground beneath the tower contains weak subsoil, which went unnoticed, and was worsened by plans to include a mere eight foot foundation for the nearly two-hundred foot tall building. Within four years the tower began to lean; it's a small miracle it actually survived construction.

While we smirk at Pisano's mistake, his flawed thinking resembles our culture. We too love instant results and quick fame; we focus on external appearance, often to the neglect of the foundation underneath. Transformations such as Jason's will never stand on a weak foundation. Quick fixes are ubiquitous to Western culture, and often lead to the same results.

Think about it. Almost all advertising entices us to believe a quick fix will solve our chronic problems. The $500 billion fast food industry is built around this idea. Even the name "fast food" perfectly summarizes the concept and it has transformed our expectations of food. I once found myself frustrated in a drive-thru line because my food was two minutes late – two minutes of my life I will never get back! But my righteous indignation was abruptly interrupted by a reality check: My ancestors toiled over barren fields in order to store enough food to last through a harsh winter … while I'm here mentally berating someone because my french fries are slightly cold. I embraced the rebuke and instead resolved to enjoy my now soggy potatoes, albeit only with modest success.

The lottery is perhaps the apex of the quick-fix mentality. What better solution to longstanding poverty than instant, unearned riches? I've experienced its allure firsthand. While in high school, my friends and I were broke. We needed to get home, but collectively produced a mere dollar in gas money. It was just enough to make it. But not enough for ice cream. Rather than prudently filling the car up with the necessary fuel, my friend walked into the gas station and purchased a scratch off lottery ticket. He won $30, somehow violating Murphy's Law in the process, which gave us enough cash for a full tank and dessert. His indiscretion paid off.

This is the problem with the quick fix: *it works just long enough to deceive us into believing it actually leads to lasting change.* A fascinating study of lottery winners reveals that instantly winning millions of dollars does not lead to increased happiness. In fact, for many the prize is a source of pain. Why? The underlying problem of poverty is not solved by instant riches. The foundations of financial discipline and wise investing take hard work and years to develop. Adding millions of dollars to a weak fiscal foundation leads to collapse.

> THIS IS THE PROBLEM WITH THE QUICK FIX: IT WORKS JUST LONG ENOUGH TO DECEIVE US INTO BELIEVING IT ACTUALLY LEADS TO LASTING CHANGE.

Unfortunately, this problem of idolizing quick fixes extends to the Church. We also believe in fast solutions to deep-seated struggles. We prioritize external design over long-lasting foundations. Jesus warned us of this human tendency in the concluding story of His longest recorded sermon, found in Matthew 5-7.

TALE OF TWO HOUSES

Therefore everyone who hears these words of mine and puts them into practice is like a wise man who built his house on the rock. The rain came down, the streams rose, and the winds blew and beat against that house; yet it did not fall, because it had its foundation on the rock. But everyone who hears these words of mine and does not put them into practice is like a foolish man who built his house on sand. The rain came down, the streams rose, and the winds blew and beat against that house, and it fell with a great crash. Matthew 7:24-27

This passage reveals a terrifying truth: *a house built on sand won't immediately collapse*, in fact, the building will likely stand long enough to convince us it's stable. In other words, we live at risk of deceiving ourselves into believing a spiritual quick fix works permanently because it appears to stand for a season. Why take the time to find the stable rock if it appears the sand will suffice? But two things reveal a bad foundation: *time* and *trials*. Eventually they will destroy the flawed home.

Knowledge vs. Application

I grew up reading this parable, yet managed to miss the main point. I misunderstood the message to describe knowing the Word of God as the means to building a strong foundation. I was completely wrong. In reality, both people in this story know the Bible. The contrast in their outcomes resulted from their *response to the Word*, not their knowledge of it. One simply heard the message; the other actually put it into practice.

This scares me. Accumulated Bible knowledge without personal application is described by God Himself as building a house on the sand, as if constructing my own personal Leaning Tower of Pisa. The problem is widespread. Consider the global Church, what do we emphasize? Knowledge? Or Obedience? Perhaps the reason Jason's testimony is so rare stems from this unfortunate reality.

Increasing our Bible knowledge is relatively easy, especially in the technological age. Mass distribution of books, teachings, blogs, videos, and conferences lead to a stunning availability of theological knowledge. Average church members today have ready access to material unavailable even to seminary students a mere two decades ago.

But our obedience hasn't increased at the same rate. We *know* far more, yet *do* far less. In other words, the global Church is in danger of specializing in sand construction. How do we bridge the gap? How do we build deep foundations? Rather than following our flawed human instinct, let's look at the ministry model of Jesus.

THE EXAMPLE OF JESUS

The ministry model of Jesus does not make any sense. Seriously. You would never have chosen His approach and nor would I. The Bible is a shocking book yet, over time, the stories tend to grow overly familiar, which causes us to miss the radical message.

Jesus chose the most unlikely ministry strategy to build His Church. He was born in a hick village, in a backward province on the edge of the Roman Empire. He avoided the political power of Rome and the theological influence of Jerusalem for most of His ministry. Despite this, dynamic ministry options consistently presented themselves. Consider the situation and ask yourself, what would I have done?

In Mark 1:33-38, we read of Jesus healing a large number of people. He stayed up late into the evening healing an entire village, as in every single sick person. This is our greatest dream – a revival engulfing a whole area. Modern wisdom tells us to respond by buying big tents, launching nightly healing services, hosting large conferences, and topping it all off by penning a bestselling book. Yet Jesus' response blows me away. The next morning He awoke early and simply left.

This is shocking. It doesn't make any sense to our modern minds, nor did it to the disciples. We exclaim, "Everyone is looking for you!" Yet Jesus replies, "I have a better plan." His counterintuitive ministry extended beyond this one story.

Consider the feeding of the 5,000, the one miracle story described in each of the Gospel accounts. Thousands of people experienced Jesus' power firsthand to meet their needs. Predictably, this left a deep impression, and John 6:15 described the electric atmosphere following the supernatural meal. The people understood that they had witnessed true spiritual power and responded by seeking to extend it politically by making Jesus king.

Imagine receiving an unexpected phone call from an unknown number. You pick up to hear a stern voice. It's a powerful senator informing you that Congress just declared you the new President. The Marine One helicopter is on the way. How would you respond? Surely this is your calling! It is an open door from the Lord for dynamic ministry, a powerful chance to shape culture for a generation. Yet Jesus, faced with this very scenario, responded by retreating to the desert. Again, this does not make sense. What was His better plan?

Rather than embrace these opportunities, Jesus inaugurated the Church by finding a small town and selecting rough, blue collar workers (along with the occasional political extremist and white collar criminal) to be His core. His approach prioritized life-on-life discipleship with a few average people, people like us, rather than the quick fix of political or spiritual notoriety. Maybe we should take note.

The small discipleship process Jesus initiated continues today, 2,000 years later. His Kingdom is still advancing. Today nearly one billion people have put their faith in Christ. The Church is growing and spreading across the world, while the contemporary power structures of Jesus' day faded away long ago. The Roman Empire is a history lesson. The Temple in Jerusalem is an archeology site. But the Church is still changing the world.

I find it a poignant indictment of our culture that we've redefined the word "movement" to now refer to a trendy marketing campaign, calling its loyal adherents to temporary online activism – all from the comfort of their top-end smartphone. Let's stop deceiving ourselves into thinking that a trending topic on social media actually leads to any lasting change. Real movements require real sacrifice, and real movements lead to real transformation. It's time for us to rediscover our main calling.

OUR MISSION

Jesus modeled discipleship, intentionally rejecting opportunities we consider more powerful and influential. He also commanded us to disciple others. How do we build strong foundations? *By reprioritizing discipleship as our primary ministry approach.* This does not negate the need for us to exercise our spiritual gifts, but instead restores Kingdom balance by putting discipleship first.

Teaching is wonderful and is listed as one of the gifts described in Ephesians 4:11. The gift of healing is much needed in the body of Christ and is mentioned as a manifestation of the Spirit in 1 Corinthians 12:9. In addition to spiritual gifts, the world desperately needs godly men and women to serve in politics, following the example of Nicodemus. But without a foundation of discipleship, none of these things will produce lasting change.

If we pursue knowledge, spiritual experiences, or societal impact apart from discipleship, then we are chasing a quick fix. With a base of discipleship, these gifts add a great depth to the mission of the Church. Without such a base, these gifts deceive us into thinking the Church is strong when, in reality, either time or trials will soon reveal our fatal flaw. Let's embrace this mission from God to His Church. If we want His results, then let us consider doing ministry His way.

> *IF WE PURSUE KNOWLEDGE, SPIRITUAL EXPERIENCES, OR SOCIETAL IMPACT APART FROM DISCIPLESHIP, THEN WE ARE CHASING A QUICK FIX.*

The Great Commission

Embracing the mission of Jesus requires us to change, as His disciples quickly discovered. One month shook their entire world. For years they followed Jesus as He led the ministry and built His Church. They assumed His ministry existed as a precursor to the establishment of a new Jewish kingdom, only to find their worldview shattered with the death, burial, and resurrection of their Master. Before they even fully processed this fundamental shift, Jesus ascended up into the clouds. I can only imagine the sobriety of this holy moment. The baton of God's rescue mission passed on to them. To us.

His last words describe the mission statement of the Church: "Go, make disciples of all the nations." In other words, Jesus delegated His shockingly counter-intuitive ministry approach to the Church. It's really not complicated, but it is really difficult. Discipleship is messy and painful. Discipleship requires full participation from the church body, not just the professional clergy. Discipleship often fails to produce either quick or measurable results. As a result, we've focused on other giftings and other missions – though not necessarily bad ones – yet failed to accomplish the one primary Mission given to us.

Imagine a global Church built on a foundation of discipleship! All the other gifts would blossom: teaching leading to greater depth, pastoring facilitating greater healing, and social engagement causing lasting transformation. Let's reclaim our calling. If we do, I'm convinced we will see the same results the Church has always seen, the same results as the Early Church portrayed in the Book of Acts.

The Example of the Early Church

When you think of the word "church," what comes to mind? Buildings? Pews? Felt boards? Committees? None of these are inherently bad, well maybe felt boards, but neither do they define a biblical church. The Book of Acts describes the Early Church, with Acts 2:42-47 vividly revealing how the first disciples sought to live out their Mission.

> *They devoted themselves to the apostles' teaching and to fellowship, to the breaking of bread and to prayer. Everyone was filled with awe at the many wonders and signs performed by the apostles. All the believers were together and had everything in common. They sold property and possessions to give to anyone who had need. Every day they continued to meet together in the temple courts. They broke bread in their homes and ate together with glad and sincere hearts, praising God and enjoying the favor of all the people. And the*

Lord added to their number daily those who were being saved. Acts 2:42-47

The first believers experienced God's presence, they grew in God's Word, and they consistently saw people added to their number. They met in a large group setting at the temple, but equally importantly they met house-to-house. Early Christians lived in deep discipleship community, so much so that "membership" in the church appeared to be those who met in houses, not those who listened to the temple sermons. Discipleship community was set as the foundation for church life, not an optional program for the most committed.

And as a result, they lived in constant awe. They daily saw people added to their number. Soon the city took notice, and within a generation, they touched the entire known world.

Your Calling

Not all of us preach. Not everyone is gifted to serve in politics. Only a small percentage of Christians will ever serve in vocational ministry, but everyone is called to make disciples. Businessmen and women, teachers, stay-at-home moms and dads, politicians, and retail clerks all inherit the same foundational mission: to make disciples.

Ten dynamic leaders will make an impact on a city, but no matter their talent, their legacy has a limit. No person is given limitless capacity. Yours may be far-reaching or it may feel painfully insignificant. Regardless of your capability, you can make disciples. Maybe it's your children, maybe it's a neighbor or co-worker, or maybe you have grace to disciple ten people. The number doesn't matter. What counts is every person playing their part, every believer in the game. Addition will never reach a city, but multiplication has no limit. You disciple two, who disciple two more, who in turn do the same. Eventually, this multiplies far beyond your limited capacity. But the Mission only works when everyone embraces his or her calling.

The Power of Discipleship in Small Groups

At Antioch Community Church, where I have served for thirteen years, we believe community is an integral aspect of discipleship. Many churches utilize small groups in order to provide a place of community for members; likewise, many churches develop a discipleship path for spiritual growth. But my experience is that these are often separated. *It is our belief that discipleship works best when combined together with community.* In fact, I don't think effective discipleship is possible outside of authentic community. Likewise, I do not believe church community is sustainable apart from discipleship.

Remember Jason's story? As per his own reflections, while he walked through a formal curriculum for new believers, these lessons were helpful but a minor part of his overall experience. The intangibles of consistent community instead served as the driving force for his transformation. And his story is not unique. Many others have experienced a similar change through these communities.

At Antioch, we primarily facilitate discipleship community through our small groups, which we call Lifegroups. We seek to create deep relationships within the church for every member, but fellowship alone is not our ultimate goal. Discipleship is our main calling. In fact, we describe discipleship as our "X Factor," which means that if given the choice to limit everything to only one ministry activity, we'd choose life-on-life discipleship. The term Lifegroup is used throughout this book to describe the venue for discipleship. Most chapters focus on the actual life-on-life process of making disciples but, because of the importance of the small group, the book will also address the practical aspects of Lifegroup leadership.

While Lifegroups function as the primary structure for discipleship, we desire for the Great Commission to spread far beyond our church walls. We train Lifegroup leaders to facilitate discipleship within their group, but our goal is that each group member in turn seeks to make disciples within their unique sphere of influence in the community. Groups are vital for discipleship, but discipleship should never be limited to groups. They are the starting point, and thus a critical aspect of training, but to truly reach a city, discipleship must spread beyond any one church.

The Antioch model is not perfect; in fact, much of this material stems from knowledge gained through our mistakes. Though you may never lead a Lifegroup or your church may utilize small groups differently, you are still called to make disciples. The primary goal of this book is to empower discipleship, with an emphasis on Lifegroups. The biblical principle of discipleship will work in any model of ministry, even if the application points may vary.

Ultimately, we stand at a critical junction in history when the Church needs to rediscover her calling. Imagine the impact of every believer in every church fully living on mission to their community. Imagine the power of true discipleship defining the church experience, not an aberration for a lucky few. People would change, families would be restored, and businesses would look different. Add this all up together and we'd see communities radically transformed. Jason's testimony created a movement, and I'm jealous for hundreds, even thousands, of more stories just like it.

The Early Church experienced a discipleship revolution, the Reformation saw a similar transformation, and even in our nation's limited history we've seen this type of revival. And we desperately need it again. You play a significant role. Embrace your call to make disciples and don't give up; years later you will turn around and see an expanding wake of transformation.

NEXT STEPS

This book seeks to empower you to make disciples. You will learn what makes a great Lifegroup leader and disciple-maker. You will discover ways to lead others in spiritual growth and to care for pastoral needs. You will also learn to facilitate the actual Lifegroup meeting. The topics range from deeply spiritual to inherently practical but everything points to one goal – to make disciples. To conclude this chapter, let's go back to the Great Commission. This passage imparts a mission to the Church, but also provides critical steps toward seeing it accomplished. Take a few minutes to answer the following questions, which we will revisit throughout the rest of the book.

> *Then Jesus came to them and said, "All authority in heaven and on earth has been given to me. Therefore go and make disciples of all nations, baptizing them in the name of the Father and of the Son and of the Holy Spirit, and teaching them to obey everything I have commanded you. And surely I am with you always, to the very end of the age." Matthew 28:18-20*

Questions

List the two promises found in this passage. If we genuinely believe them to be true, how would that affect our perspective on leading Lifegroup and discipling others?

List the four commands found in this passage. How does this compare to your answer above? What is the typical application of these commands in the Church? Do they reflect the Great Commission, or something different?

The final command is "teach them to obey," yet we often reduce it to "teach." List out typical teaching methods in one column and methods for teaching to obey in a separate column. What should you emphasize in order to lead a group that "teaches to obey"?

CHAPTER 2

Your Role

---

*All authority in heaven and on earth has been given
to me. Therefore... And surely I am with you always,
to the very end of the age.*

For my sixteenth birthday, I was initiated into the driving public by receiving a decade-old minivan. Faux wood side panels graced the exterior, complete with the added benefit of forced humility for my teenage self. The tape deck mostly destroyed cassettes, which didn't matter much since I only owned CDs. The rear-view mirror was missing and a side mirror later tragically decapitated by a telephone pole. Rather predictably, the car did not survive the year.

I upgraded with my next vehicle. I still remember driving to a dealership on the other side of town to purchase the small hatchback, complete with ironically imprinted racing stripes and the number nine. But I ran into a complication. Somehow in the purchasing process, I failed to realize the car contained a manual transmission.

For two hours, I drove the surrounding neighborhood seeking to master the shift from first to second gear. Right as my confidence began to increase, I heard a clanking noise and discovered the gears no longer changed. Apparently my driving lesson burned out the clutch. I limped back to the dealer and discovered the cost of fixing the part was actually greater than the price of the car. Rather than sink money into a mistake, I cut my losses and moved on, eventually landing in the luxury of a Buick.

My car woes taught me two great lessons: The first being that minivans and Buicks have a negative effect on the dating life of a high schooler. The second showed me that a failure to properly change gears always leads to burnout. Gears allow the car to increase speed exponentially, without necessarily increasing the pressure on the engine. Increased acceleration apart from a gearshift will cause the engine to red-line. It simply cannot go faster; the added force only results in exhaustion.

I've discovered leaders generally do not switch gears naturally, and, similar to my ill-fated racer, the result is burnout. Burnout stems from viewing increasing labor as the solution to every problem. Driving in one gear is possible, but constrained by a limit: your personal capacity. It is possible for leaders to thrive in their responsibility, but they must learn to shift gears.

This principle applies to virtually any leadership role, but is especially relevant for disciple-makers. Many work a full-time job, seek to disciple their children, and serve in the community in addition to this responsibility. Three specific gears are fundamentally important to sustain effective discipleship: prayer, modeling, and delegation. By utilizing these tools, your impact is multiplied far beyond your capacity and your energy. Without them, I believe you will eventually start to red-line. Mastering the gears takes practice and is worth every moment.

QUALITIES OF GREAT LIFEGROUP LEADERS

They Pray

I once discipled a man who recently escaped a lifestyle of drugs and alcohol. He joined my group and we met consistently for months – that is until he suddenly stopped taking my calls. I tried to reach him, yet simply couldn't get through. I knew he relapsed into his old habits but felt powerless to help. All I knew to do was pray. I prayed for him consistently for months, asking God to intervene and get his attention. To be honest, my faith was low.

I received a call out of the blue months later from my friend asking to meet up. He looked visibly shaken the next day as we met. He described attending a party the previous night, drinking heavily and eventually ending up in the bathroom. But as he vomited up his excess, the power of God descended upon the room. He lay on the floor for hours, sobered and shaking in holy fear. He repented under the conviction of God. The experience marked him, still evident the next day, and catalyzed a turning point in his life.

His confession floored me. I discovered prayer carries greater power than I ever realized. I made a commitment to make prayer a central role in discipleship. I have limits to my power, but God does not. We cannot mold another person into Christ's image. We cannot cause spiritual revelation, nor create true conviction. These are works of the Spirit alone, and He invites us to partner in prayer.

Pray for your Lifegroup and those you disciple, and pray for individuals by name. Start a prayer journal and list out specific requests for each person. Even consider doing this for the whole group. If you hit a roadblock within the group, invest time in intercession. I often catch myself spending far more time worrying about problems than praying for solutions. Above all, recognize the answer to problems stems from the power of God far more than it does from your increased efforts.

They Model

Think of someone who influenced you in a profound way. What caused the influence? Was it their achievements? Their credentials? Their words? Or was it their actions? Most people will describe the person's lifestyle far more than any other factor as the reason for the lasting impact.

Simply put, we value actions over words. Discipleship creates an environment to model our lifestyle, whether we like it or not. People will see you, your interactions with others, and your good and bad days. Preachers and authors may promote ideals, but disciple-makers live these values in real life.

This gear intimidates me more than the others; it's easier to tell someone what to do than it is to apply the same truth to my own life. No one perfectly lives Kingdom values; we all travel together in the journey toward Christ-likeness. But we do set the tempo. People see your hunger, they see your transparency. They witness you aspiring to lead your family, confessing your own sin, disciplining yourself to seek God, and choosing integrity at work. These actions create a powerful impression.

When identifying great Lifegroup leaders and disciple-makers, often the defining characteristic is their lifestyle, not their hours spent in preparation. Commit to seek God as your first priority. Before you invest any time in facilitating a group meeting, first ensure your own devotional life is consistent, your own marriage is healthy, and that you are walking on the path to holiness. If you commit to these basics, you'll discover people listing your name as the answer to our original question.

They Delegate

"Work yourself out of a job" was my first job description as a newly minted Lifegroup leader and disciple-maker. It later proved to be some of the wisest advice I've received. When dialoguing with leaders on the edge of burnout, I almost inevitably discover they carry virtually every aspect of the group. They always host, they buy snacks, they organize the kid's rotation, they lead worship, they facilitate discussion, and they send all the reminders. I'm tired just listening to them.

It doesn't have to be this way. *The best leaders do the least and empower the most.* But we face a big hurdle to shifting into this gear: Delegation requires an initial investment in order to realize a later return. Most people find it easier to go with the status quo of doing everything themselves; that is, until they burn out. We do everything until we run out of energy, and then respond by doing nothing.

While this third gear applies primarily to those who make disciples by leading a small group, this principle still extends even to one-on-one discipleship. You may not feel the tension as acutely, but you need to recognize that any one-sided relationship will burn you out over time.

List out every role required for the group. How many require your direct involvement? Start by listing the roles causing you the most stress. Which group member would be a better fit for that role? If you personally fill all the roles, you rob other members of the chance to serve the group. While I believe the underlying motivation for this behavior is service, the destructive habit actually limits the group. I've been shocked to discover my most burdensome

> DISCIPLESHIP CREATES AN ENVIRONMENT TO MODEL OUR LIFESTYLE, WHETHER WE LIKE IT OR NOT.

responsibilities become someone else's greatest joy. This is why God gives us different gifts. This is why He created us as a body, comprised of many parts.

Create a rotation for consistent Lifegroup responsibilities as a starting point. Include snacks, host home, and any childcare needs. Consider training members to take on additional aspects of the groups, such as worship, discussion, or communication. To delegate these latter functions, you will need to invest time training and coaching, but the result will allow your group to do far more, and it will cost you far less.

Wherever possible, I encourage Lifegroup leaders to develop co-leaders to share the burden of responsibility. Even without official co-leaders, you can still distribute the work, freeing yourself and increasing ownership among the group in the process.

QUALIFICATIONS OF LEADERSHIP

Character

The above traits mark great leaders, but we must also recognize biblical qualifications for leadership. At times, people need to first resolve a character issue prior to leading. That being said, no leader is perfect. We all have areas in which we need to grow. The goal for a leader in regard to their character is direction, not perfection.

Jason certainly had not mastered the list below before he began making disciples, but he was committed to the destination and teachable in his weaknesses. The way a leader lives his or her life and the character with which they conduct themselves will make a far greater impact than anything that is ever said. Overwhelmingly, the biblical standard for a leader is NOT experience or training, but character.

> *Here is a trustworthy saying: Whoever aspires to be an overseer desires a noble task. Now the overseer is to be above reproach, faithful to his wife, temperate, self-controlled, respectable, hospitable, able to teach, not given to drunkenness, not violent but gentle, not quarrelsome, not a lover of money. He must manage his own family well and see that his children obey him, and he must do so in a manner worthy of full respect. (If anyone does not know how to manage his own family,*

how can he take care of God's church?) He must not be a recent convert, or he may become conceited and fall under the same judgment as the devil. He must also have a good reputation with outsiders, so that he will not fall into disgrace and into the devil's trap.

In the same way, deacons are to be worthy of respect, sincere, not indulging in much wine, and not pursuing dishonest gain. They must keep hold of the deep truths of the faith with a clear conscience. They must first be tested; and then if there is nothing against them, let them serve as deacons.

In the same way, the women are to be worthy of respect, not malicious talkers but temperate and trustworthy in everything.

A deacon must be faithful to his wife and must manage his children and his household well. Those who have served well gain an excellent standing and great assurance in their faith in Christ Jesus. 1 Timothy 3:1-13

Many churches and ministries have fallen apart because of leaders falling into sin. These anointed men and women labored for the Kingdom for years, but because of hidden sin in their lives, destroyed the very thing they sought to build. None of us, regardless of our position of leadership, is beyond sin, but through the Holy Spirit, we can all walk in freedom.

Leaders must always stay accountable. It is a tragic tendency of leaders to see themselves as "above the law" and have no outside input into their personal lives. James 1:13-15 describes the cycle of sin that affects all mankind: *"Let no one say when he is tempted, 'I am being tempted by God,' for God cannot be tempted with evil, and he himself tempts no one. But each person is tempted when he is lured and enticed by his own desire. Then desire when it has conceived gives birth to sin, and sin when it is fully grown brings forth death."*

Temptation affects all of us, but there is a way out. James 5:16 states, *"Therefore, confess your sins to one another and pray for one another, that you may be healed."* Though it may start small and insignificant, if we do not confess our sins and deal with them, the hidden sin in our lives will grow and eventually cause destruction.

We should honor one another's giftings, but never at the expense of character. I believe the spiritual health of disciple-makers and Lifegroup leaders is far more important than the role they fill. These biblical standards describe God's criteria for leadership. The qualifications should exist in a grace-based environment for each person to confess sin and find healing, even leaders. That being said, at Antioch Community Church, if a leader is unable to walk in freedom from sin, we will ask him or her to step down for a season to find healing for their own soul, not as a punishment but rather as an opportunity for healing. We highly encourage your church to do the same.

In addition to the 1 Timothy list, other biblical passages reveal critical leadership traits. Read the following and consider how these apply to your life.

> *You know that the rulers of the Gentiles lord it over them and their high officials exercise authority over them. Not so with you. Instead, whoever wants to become great among you must be your servant, and whoever wants to be first must be your slave.*
> Matthew 20:25

> *You, my brothers, were called to be free. But do not use your freedom to indulge the sinful nature; rather, serve one another in love.* Galatians 5:13

> *"Everything is permissible"—but not everything is beneficial. "Everything is permissible"—but not everything*

*is constructive. Nobody should seek his own good, but
the good of others.* 2 Corinthians 10:23-24

*Do not destroy the work of God for the sake of food. All
food is clean, but it is wrong for a man to eat anything
that causes someone else to stumble. It is better not to
eat meat or drink wine or to do anything else that will
cause your brother to fall.* Romans 14:20-21

These traits represent just a handful of what defines biblical
leadership. It's nearly impossible to list everything needed; instead,
I challenge any Lifegroup leader or disciple-maker to pursue God's
Word as the standard of leadership and to allow His Spirit to convict
you and mold you into the image of Christ. Commit to transparency
and humility, even with your failure. Let's walk together in the steps
of Jesus and trust in that doing so, we will blaze a trail for others.

As a practical application point, I suggest you also consider
your church and community's culture when evaluating standards for
Lifegroup leaders or disciple-makers. For example, at Antioch Community Church, we ask leaders to avoid personal "gray areas" at any
Lifegroup function due to the uniqueness of each member's life. For
us, this means that alcohol should never be a part of any Lifegroup
event and any media should be entirely above reproach.

The Commitment of a Leader

Discipleship is an ongoing process, but like anything in life, there is
a natural lifecycle. As such, I recommend defining the commitment
length for any particular group or discipleship relationship. Discipleship is a life-long progression of spiritual growth, but your particular
part in someone else's spiritual growth will be limited.

I suggest a shorter initial commitment that can be extended
instead of a long commitment, which you may need to break. It's
much less painful to re-initiate a group than it is to end a group

prematurely (though an unfortunate necessity at times). For new discipleship groups or one-on-one relationships, I typically commit to nine months as a starting point. For a Lifegroup, I recommend leaders make a minimum commitment of one year.

Churches should also prayerfully clarify other expectations of their Lifegroup leaders. Every church is a family, and all families ask for commitments from their various members. In my home, my kids – even the toddler – have chores and responsibilities. It's part of what makes us family; while I don't always love doing the dishes, I am nevertheless deeply grateful for a place to belong. Church is no different. At my church, we determined Lifegroup leaders must be members of the church since they hold pastoral responsibility, and leaders are expected to regularly attend church in order to stay connected with our larger spiritual family.

We ask Lifegroup leaders to commit to leading for a year, generally from August to August, while fully recognizing situations emerge that require unexpected transitions. We also ask leaders to attend a monthly Lifegroup leader meeting, generally during one of our services on Sunday morning, as well as an annual Lifegroup rally.

COMMIT TO TRANSPARENCY AND HUMILITY, EVEN WITH YOUR FAILURE. LET'S WALK TOGETHER IN THE STEPS OF JESUS AND TRUST IN THAT DOING SO, WE WILL BLAZE A TRAIL FOR OTHERS.

Furthermore, for leaders of groups with children, we ask leaders to undergo a background check. Unfortunately, given the prevalence of sin in our culture, we need to strive even harder to live above reproach, and we believe this serves as a necessary safeguard.

Your church may ask for additional commitments from its leaders. Don't begrudge the responsibility, instead celebrate the fact that you are placed in a spiritual family and given a place of contribution.

UNDERSTAND YOUR PLACE

I once led a Deathgroup, perhaps the worst Lifegroup in my church's history. Every guy I sought to disciple left. The group shrunk in half almost immediately, and within a year reduced to just four and a half members. One didn't talk and another only spoke Spanish, which no one else in the group knew. And we don't talk about the half member. Yet it was my best year of leading. I lived every ideal, embraced every best practice for leaders. I interceded for the group daily, diligently prepared every week, and creatively sought multiple new outreach opportunities. And none of it mattered. My group fell apart.

Our spring outreach marked the low point. I cast bold vision for each member to invite unchurched friends to our cookout in a local park. I also knew the tendency of our group toward inaction so I built in a failsafe back-up. We cooked a large amount of fajitas; if no lost friends arrived, then we planned to give out free food to others in the park and share the gospel. A beautiful plan.

But I didn't anticipate the rain. Right as the meat turned a golden brown over the grill, a fat raindrop hit my face. The park emptied immediately. No lost friends, no people in sight. Yet rather than admit defeat, I hung up a tarp in the tree and huddled alongside the two other members, silently eating our bountiful supply of Mexican food in the cold rain. I decided perhaps leadership wasn't my best fit. God taught me a powerful lesson: success doesn't depend on me. Despite the challenge, this revelation set me free.

The commands of the Great Commission are bookended by promises. Jesus holds all authority and He is with us always. Therefore, we go. The word "therefore" links the promise with the command, and I believe this is the difference between striving and rest in leadership.

I only go because Jesus has all authority. It's His power at work that enables me to step out and make disciples. There is no other way. Imagine the freedom if we truly believed this promise. We'd no longer pressure ourselves to produce results; instead when faced with challenges, we'd seek God and wait for Him to move. *We still work hard, but our labor doesn't define our identity.*

Matthew 11:28-30 describes God's yoke as easy and His burden light. We read the passage, nod our heads in agreement, but often fail to see its relevance in our lives. In theory, it is easy to believe God wants us to have rest and life. In practice, the more responsibility we are given, the wearier we become. Tiredness is not necessarily bad, but consistent spiritual weariness is an indicator something is wrong with the way you carry the burden.

Since the John Deere long ago replaced the yoke, we struggle to understand the passage. What once was an easily understood analogy has been lost in a modern, urban culture. Yokes hold two oxen together to plow a field, allowing the farmer to harness the power of two animals. The yoke keeps them moving in the same direction; otherwise the entirety of the weight would fall on one.

Jesus tells us His *yoke* is easy. Notice He did not say His *mission* is easy. And for good reason, it isn't; in fact, His mission is impossible. There is simply no way for us to carry it out. Instead, His yoke is easy, meaning He is strong enough to bear the burden as long as we remain in step with Him. When we learn to abide and to live by the Spirit, we come under the yoke of Jesus. No longer do we carry the burden on our own. Instead, we allow Him to carry it for us. Our responsibility is to simply stay connected to Him. Far too often, believers embrace the mission of God and race out into the harvest field to plow on their own, a guaranteed pathway to burnout.

Let's diligently develop the qualities of great leaders. Let's embrace the qualifications of biblical leaders, and let's recognize our place, staying in step with Jesus. If we commit to these, we will witness God multiply disciples, and we will thrive in the process.

Spiritual Growth Exercise

Describe the spiritual journey that prompted you to lead.

From the list in 1 Timothy 3, where do you feel you are the strongest? Where do you most need to grow?

How will you prioritize your relationship with Jesus in the midst of serving others?

Which of the three indicators (prayer, modeling, delegation) is most natural for you? Most difficult?

Is there anything you feel needs to be resolved in your life prior to leading?

Are you able to embrace the commitment of leading a group?

CHAPTER 3

Define Your Group

"Go"

I wanted to quit. Fresh on the heels of my ill-fated Deathgroup outreach, I determined leading Lifegroup wasn't for me. At one level, I learned the lesson that God alone brings growth, but the pain of leading a dying group sapped whatever vision remained. *My vision* by *my strength* proved an ineffective formula. It was time to resign.

One week later it all changed. I was protesting my situation in prayer, my pleas woven with a confused mixture of frustration and surrender. I expressed my anger and confessed my ambition. In the quiet aftermath of my complaints, I sensed the Lord speak, "I'm going to send you five men. Disciple them." That's it. But this quiet response instilled a fresh resolve as I embraced a vision that neither originated in nor depended upon me.

My resignation was rejected and in its place a vision imparted. Leadership brought fresh life to my soul, even though my circumstances had yet to change.

The groups I've led generally wind down in the summer due to the culture of our city. In this particular summer, I maximized this lull to intercede for my new calling from God. Though my Lifegroup appeared to barely survive on life-support, internally I felt a deep sense of purpose. I left envisioned to see this group develop a culture of discipleship and even become a training ground for future missionaries.

Within nine months I was discipling five men. These five served as the catalyst for the Lifegroup growing to thirty people. We multiplied into two Lifegroups the following year and then again in the next. Within several years, this original core served as the foundation for ten Lifegroups and nearly two hundred people. Two international church plants were launched from the first waves of people brought into the group. It all started with a Deathgroup and a vision.

A clear sense of purpose is perhaps the most critical ingredient for a group. A defining purpose becomes the catalyst for fresh life; without it, direction is reduced to reactive leadership.

GO

The first command of the Great Commission tells us to *go*. The word implies action and movement, yet for many believers we instead expect the unchurched to *come* to us. *Going* is uncomfortable regardless of whether the location is across the street, the cubicle, or the world, but only in doing so do we experience the life found in living on mission.

> *GOING IS UNCOMFORTABLE REGARDLESS OF WHETHER THE LOCATION IS ACROSS THE STREET, THE CUBICLE, OR THE WORLD, BUT ONLY IN DOING SO DO WE EXPERIENCE THE LIFE FOUND IN LIVING ON MISSION.*

The Greek word "Go" in this passage was originally written in participle form; "As you are going" is perhaps a better translation. *Going* does not necessarily require us to leave our location but rather challenges us to live on mission where we already are. The Church's mission must extend to all nations, but your part might primarily focus on your neighborhood.

The delegation of the Great Commission to a few professionals limits the spread of the Gospel more than perhaps any other deception. We need to rediscover our calling to fulfill the Great Commission; we need to reject the lie that only trained pastors make disciples. When we rediscover our calling to be Kingdom ambassadors, anything is possible.

Rediscover Your Calling

All this is from God, who reconciled us to himself through Christ and gave us the ministry of reconciliation: that God was reconciling the world to himself in Christ, not counting people's sins against them. And he has committed to us the message of reconciliation. We are therefore Christ's ambassadors, as though God were making his appeal through us. 2 Corinthians 5:19-20

India is unmistakably foreign to Westerners; every sense is vividly assaulted by a beautiful array of sights, smells, and tastes. These reflections floated through my mind as I gazed out the taxi window while slowing weaving toward the center of Mumbai Peninsula, which serves as the home for twenty million people.

My destination was the United States Consulate. Forty-five minutes later, my ride abruptly ended outside the non-descript wall of a former maharaja's palace. I walked past a few bored guards at the gate and into an elaborate security procedure, which eventually deposited me into a quiet courtyard and en route to a waiting room.

As I stepped inside, I found the atmosphere change from the swarming streets of Mumbai into the stillness of the consulate to be stunning. Everything felt like home, the staff even expertly captured the 1950-esque smell of an American rural post office. It dawned on me – I just crossed the threshold from one kingdom into another. This is an ambassador's job.

The significance of the word "ambassador" should not be lost on us. Ambassadors receive a commission to represent their Kingdom to another; it's a position of high honor and high responsibility. Do we live our calling? When co-workers step into your office do they experience the same stunning atmosphere change? Do neighbors recognize the transition from one kingdom into another when they cross the threshold of your doorway?

Reach Your Sphere of Influence

Everyone has a sphere of influence. It's unique to you – a combination of your social network, occupation, family, and geography. While some are entrusted with a large influence, most people's circle is modest. And it doesn't matter at all. The size of your sphere of influence exerts no sway over your calling. Some ambassadors reach China, others the Maldives. The responsibility looks different but the commission is the same.

You are an ambassador to your sphere of influence; it's your primary occupation, regardless of the title on your business card. You are not "just" a teacher, but rather an ambassador to your school; not "just" a retail clerk, instead an ambassador to the store. Imagine the impact of each one of us embracing our calling! God positions His ambassadors across the city in stores, schools, neighborhoods, and businesses – but will we do our part? If so, there are more than enough Kingdom agents positioned to see cities transformed. We've seen this occur in several places across our city, Waco, Texas.

Mark, an Antioch Discipleship School student, found part-time employment as a barista for a coffee chain. He had no ambition to launch a career making lattes. He just sought to pay the bills. Despite the temporary arrangement, Mark recognized his primary calling was to be an ambassador, and this store represented his current assignment.

In response, he resolved to be a great employee. Mark showed up on time and worked diligently. He labored to establish a positive environment of encouragement during every shift, seeking to create an embassy of Heaven behind the counter. People noticed. After observing his effect on co-workers, his boss soon promoted him to "Director of Employee Morale" ... not a typical coffee shop job description.

Mark's impact grew so dynamic that the manager's husband remarked he knew whether or not Mark worked on a given day based upon his wife's mood when she returned home. Multiple employees accepted Christ through his influence of both lifestyle and words. Ambassadors change the atmosphere.

Others brought similar impact to different parts of our community. Brandon took a sales position with a local firm and within a few months he began to gather weekly with a few co-workers to pray before work. In addition to fervent prayer, they committed to unwavering integrity and they prioritized the needs of people over the lure of quick riches. At first nothing changed. In fact, their decision caused tension as some in management began to express concern about their overt spirituality.

But after a year of perseverance, business contracts started to land. Clients felt genuinely cared for, the team felt a close bonding, and soon they were among the most profitable unit in the business; so much so that management regularly sought out their secret. The word began to spread. Other employees began to show up before work to share life struggles; clients started to call in prayer requests, even referring friends across the country also experiencing life crises. All this led to both a steady stream of salvation and a blessed business. Again, ambassadors change the atmosphere.

Lead Your Group

Every believer is an ambassador charged with making disciples within their unique appointment. Lifegroup leaders need to seek their personal calling, but must expand their vision to define the broader mission of the group. Often these are closely linked. You cannot define your group's vision without first embracing your personal calling.

I've noticed many leaders on the edge of burnout due to a perceived discrepancy between personal calling and Lifegroup vision. This separation is unnecessary. Are you a young family? Then reach other young families. Do you have a passion for business? Then reach the business community with your group. Lifegroup works best when the variety of groups reflect the variety of people within the church, and ultimately within the broader community.

The community where I live is diverse, as is my church. No one group will reach everyone. But everyone can still be reached if we each do our part. At Antioch Waco, we've launched over a hundred adult Lifegroups, each with a different flavor. One group launched with a vision to reach blended families, the leaders each having experienced the pain of divorce and the subsequent power of healing. They developed a passion to reach others going through the same.

Another Lifegroup reached out to disconnected ethnic minority groups. Several groups built around a vision for multi-generational diversity. Some groups focused on geographic areas, others on demographic trends or shared occupations. Each vision is unique, and the more distinct the groups, the more realistic the capacity to actually reach our city.

Don't be overwhelmed by the number of groups described above. Like any other church, we started with just a few. Over time, effective discipleship resulted in more groups, which in turn, resulted in more disciples. This led to increased diversity, but it all started with a faithful few. When I consult churches, I care far more about the health of their groups than I do about the number of groups. One Lifegroup that leads to healthy reproducing discipleship will always lead to many more groups.

Your group needs a vision, a clearly defined sense of purpose. You'll encounter the resurrection of Deathgroup with the fresh life of a God-given vision. The prospect of new guests will become exciting and intercession no longer a chore. Vision is not a silver bullet for group health; things may still be difficult, but vision is a critical first step.

BUILDING A VISION

Start the process of defining your vision by answering a few questions: What has God already spoken? Where do you already have natural influence? What is it about leading that excites you? What groups of people seem under-reached in your community? As you process these questions with the Lord, a theme will start to emerge; pay attention to the feeling of fresh excitement. Generally, it's a road sign you are traveling on the correct path.

Several years ago, I felt visionless. My wife and I had one child, with another on the way, and Lifegroup felt like a routine; furthermore, we didn't seem to have a place to reach out to the lost in our city. I have worked at a church for more than a decade; our local family is all deeply connected to the church, and after fifteen years, most of my friendships originated from ministry. To compound the challenge, our busy season of life made social and athletic clubs inaccessible.

After a date one evening, my wife and I realized that we both felt burned out by Lifegroup. However, in response to this self-awareness, we didn't quit. Rather than give up, we instead set aside time to seek God for fresh purpose. Through this process it dawned on us that hundreds, if not thousands, of new people visited our church within the past year and many of them were either not yet believers or were brand new in their faith. A harvest field extended out right in front of us.

We promptly started a new Lifegroup focused on new families to the church. We established the group to be accessible for new people. We met on Sunday afternoons in order to accommodate kids' nap schedules, and we intentionally avoided insider language during the group in order to feel more welcoming to guests. We utilized regular interactions at church as opportunities to reach out. Lifegroup felt alive again. Receiving guests became exciting rather than a burden.

Over the course of six months, God sent us multiple key families, many of whom are now our closest friends.

There is always a solution. God will not call you to lead without giving you vision for where to go. It may not unfold immediately, but if you diligently seek Him then He will lead you.

Run with the Vision

Once you receive a fresh mission, start to align your group accordingly. What day of the week is the best fit? What time works? Do the lessons for kids reflect their age? As a general rule, I ask myself, "Do I enjoy my group?" If not, others probably feel the same. Go back to the drawing board when you start to feel dissatisfied; set aside time to seek God and adjust. Even consider learning from other group leaders reaching similar people and seeking God to think outside the box entirely for fresh ways to express discipleship.

As the vision takes shape, remember to communicate it regularly to the group. If you alone carry vision, then it will not take off.

Check Your Indicators

The process of determining a vision seems simple, a straightforward one-time event, but most leaders find the opposite true. Why? In short, because things change. Kids grow older and their school activities increase; some people get married while others retire. Each of these leads to a crisis of vision. What inspired yesterday may feel like a burden tomorrow. The process of defining your purpose is dynamic and requires careful attention. I find it helpful to identify warning signs to highlight a waning vision, much like the dashboard of a car.

The check engine light of my first car, the minivan, popped on one day while driving. I ignored it, unwilling to exert the energy to fix the problem. After several months, I started to hear a slight knocking sound while on the drive home from mowing lawns. My car regularly produced mystery noises so I drove on, but this time it persisted, growing louder with each passing mile. As I turned onto my street, the car sounded like a jackhammer before finally dying outside my home in a final, violent shudder as the engine gave out.

To be honest, I welcomed the van's demise, but also learned a lesson: *don't ignore your indicators*. Remember that not every indicator light represents a severe concern. For instance, every leader has a bad day, and I regularly wish to take a few weeks break from my group – regardless of how much I enjoy leading. These are natural.

But some signs point to a more serious problem. If you consistently dread your group, avoid inviting new guests, regularly look for an excuse to quit, or experience significant discord among current members then you may have a vision crisis. Create a habit to seek the Lord for fresh vision when you begin to notice these warning signs. Don't wait until a personal crisis happens to redefine purpose.

While I firmly believe we are all called to make disciples, you may discover that at times the Lord may use these warning lights to prompt you to find a different way to serve instead of Lifegroup leading. There is nothing wrong with change. Just make sure you proactively follow the Lord rather than reactively quit due to a lack of vision. I've found that every time God transitions me out of a current role He will always provide fresh vision for what is next. His vision is never just a reaction to the past.

Stay Open to People

While we embrace a clear vision and plan for outreach, we also need to acknowledge the ministry model of Jesus. He followed a clear ministry plan while on earth; in Luke 10:5 we read how He sent out the disciples with a mandate to only reach the lost sheep of Israel, a clearly defined target group. But Jesus always stood ready to embrace disruptions. He stopped His teaching for a paralyzed man descending through a roof. He rebuked His disciples for turning away children. And He ministered to a Greek woman far removed from his target group in Israel. Jesus pursued a mission, yet welcomed interruptions.

We need to exercise great care to never close ourselves off from people. I've found God consistently sends me people who may not easily fit the vision of my group. Years ago, I led a college ministry group filled with rich fraternity students and God sent me an autistic high schooler. It was wonderful. She added an important dynamic to the group; we didn't change the vision but did benefit from the diversity.

WE NEED TO EXERCISE GREAT CARE TO NEVER CLOSE OURSELVES OFF FROM PEOPLE.

I believe it's important for us all to stay open to guests who may not naturally fit. I developed a long-standing policy to say "yes" to new people. Before inviting, I may first recommend a different group that I feel will fit more naturally, especially that considering our current group has upwards of twenty kids and the discipleship is heavily focused on parenting. I warn non-parents they may not enjoy it, but they're still invited. Staying open keeps us connected to God's heart for people. I try to embrace a motto I heard from a friend who leads a different group: "There is always an empty chair."

Vision Exercise

Before moving into the next chapters, first review your vision. Evaluate the application of the next chapters through the lens of this vision. Above all, start consistently seeking God in prayer and watch Him create a path.

What is your natural sphere of influence?

What unique things has God spoken regarding your calling?

As you review the list above, create an initial vision statement for your group by answering the following: Who are you called to reach? How are you going to reach them? Why is this important?

In response to the vision statement above, consider practical elements of the group such as: When and where will the group meet? Who will you ask to partner with you? What format will you follow? Where will you position yourself to reach new people?

Take time to seek the input of your pastor or current group leader regarding the vision statement you've just created and then practice sharing it.

CHAPTER 4

Disciple Your Group

*Make disciples of all nations ... teaching them to obey
everything I have commanded you.*

Deana was excited for a much-needed fresh start. She was newly married and recently moved to a new city with her young son in order to join her husband. For the past several years, she faced numerous difficulties as a single mom and this change represented the promise of a new beginning.

But it all came crashing down shortly after her arrival. Things seemed wonderful right up until the moment she returned home to an empty house. As she walked around and noticed the missing furniture and clothes, it gradually dawned on her that her husband had left. At first she couldn't believe it. He gave no prior warning; there wasn't even a note on the counter. But reality finally hit home like a punch to the gut.

Deana sat in shock in the aftermath of this realization, unable to comprehend the magnitude of the betrayal. She was completely devastated and had never felt more alone. She didn't know anyone in this new city to help her process the pain.

Sudden loss often causes a wide range of swirling emotions as the grief of dashed dreams twist together with the memory of past hurts. For Deana, this included the painful memories of the dissolution of her prior marriage. The compounded pain rushed to the surface, and Deana reached a breaking point.

God specializes in transforming pain into grace, and for Deana, this grace arrived in the form of discipleship. All she knew to do was find a local church and reach out to community. She reluctantly joined a Lifegroup with several other women but, beyond this, she had no answers.

Throughout the Bible, we see that it's the desperate who find the greatest healing. Deana was no different. She eschewed the social norm of reserved conversation, instead choosing to pour out her heart to these new friends. She confessed her anger and sought complete transparency in her life. The other women patiently listened, prayed for their new friend, and pointed her to the Word of God. At times they shared advice but mostly they merely provided their presence.

Deana's spiritual hunger combined with the Lifegroup's support proved a potent combination. She found deep healing in the love of the Father, started the process of forgiveness, and discovered restoration in her own places of sin. While there was no definitive moment, after several months Deana was transformed into a new woman.

A few years later, a visitor walked into the group who shared a similar story and carried similar baggage. Deana realized it was now her turn to make a disciple. She reached out to this lady, sharing both her journey and her healing. Deana's story of loss and restoration developed into a powerful place of authority for someone else in need.

This story is the essence of Church. It's a vivid reminder of both earthly pain and Kingdom restoration, a perfect Father working through fragile people. Stories like this give me hope. Imagine this emerging into the normal expression of Church; consider the impact of every believer receiving this type of discipleship and healing. Then consider them turning around and investing in someone else. Rinse and repeat. These basic ingredients make up the recipe for transformation.

But the potential often goes unrealized. This type of transformation isn't complicated but it is difficult. Investing in a hurting friend requires patience; it's often not exciting. Progress is seldom a straight-line. Sure, we rejoice years later as we witness the fruit, but in the moment it feels more like one step forward and two back.

If I'm being honest, I've often felt bored leading Lifegroup; I'm not always excited to lead a discipleship group. But if I'm still honest, I strongly believe these changed my life more than anything else. It's the *consistency of discipleship community over time* which has served as the catalyst for transformation. In other words, boring things change the world. Let's face it, a conference with ten thousand people and a talented worship team is more exciting than answering accountability questions, especially when it's more or less the same conversation you've had for the last year.

We have to realize what is *most powerful* is often not the *most exciting*. This applies to just about any type of relationship. For example, good communication and healthy handling of conflict build the foundation for a thriving marriage far more than a romantic getaway. This principle takes us back to the first chapter – our obsession with quick fixes prevents us from achieving lasting change.

We need catalysts in our spiritual life, be it conferences, mission trips, or powerful times of worship, but a spark alone will not transform anyone.

SPARKS AND FUEL

I realized I wasn't an Eagle Scout one night several years ago in the middle of the Sam Houston National Forest. I assumed the process of building a fire would be easy, despite the preceding 12 hours of rain.

But I quickly discovered that wet wood doesn't easily ignite. I arrived prepared, or so I thought, with lighter fluid and plenty of matches. I spent my energy purchasing these catalysts to light the fire, but almost none actually assembling the right fuel.

I paid for my mistake. I spent a futile thirty minutes squirting lighter fluid over fledgling embers, before finally admitting defeat and eating my lukewarm hot dog, a punishment I wouldn't wish upon anyone. Pouring lighter fluid on a fire is much more exciting than gathering dry wood. It's a rush to see the flames explode upward, yet equally disappointing to see them fall back down. The fuel alone determines the strength of the fire.

Discipleship reminds me of building a fire. You need a spark, but without a solid base of fuel, the spark will never reach its potential. Before we move on and discuss the practical aspects of discipleship, let's first commit to actually do it. And let's commit to stick with it. As I reflect on fifteen years of seeking to be a disciple and striving in turn to make disciples, I truly believe the most significant quality has been the simplicity of continuing to show up. That's it. And yet that's a lot harder than most of us think.

THE PROCESS

The command to *make disciples* is the only imperative in the Great Commission; the other verbs are all participles. This is a geeky way of saying our mission is to *make disciples* and we do it by going, baptizing, and teaching to obey. In other words, if we don't *make disciples* then we've entirely missed the point, regardless of how far we go or how many we've baptized.

IF WE DON'T *MAKE DISCIPLES* THEN WE'VE ENTIRELY MISSED THE POINT, REGARDLESS OF HOW FAR WE GO OR HOW MANY WE'VE BAPTIZED.

Discipleship Defined

Making disciples is a direct command from Jesus Christ to His Church. In other words, it's a big deal, so I believe it's prudent to define a few terms:

A *Disciple* is a person who looks like the One they follow, a person who looks like Jesus.

Discipleship is one person helping another become a lifelong, obedient, and reproducing follower of Jesus.

We never attempt to make disciples of ourselves – that's just weird – rather, we labor to see disciples of Jesus multiplied. However, we unashamedly believe the way this happens is through life-on-life investment. Our spiritual growth is not an individual sport. We need each other.

As stated earlier, at Antioch Waco, Lifegroups function as the structure to provide discipleship to our church. As a basic standard, *we want every Lifegroup to have corresponding men's and women's discipleship groups.* These groups may gather as part of the Lifegroup night, either by splitting the night in half or through a rotation, or they may meet at a separate time during the week. This chapter describes the process of leading a discipleship group, either as part of a Lifegroup or separately out in the community.

Due to the relational depth inherent in the discipleship process, discipleship relationships should be limited to the same gender. In addition to this principle, there are several different ways to organize discipleship. Regardless of the approach you utilize, remember that consistency is more important than perfection.

I generally encourage group discipleship rather than one-on-one. For starters, Jesus modeled group discipleship, albeit with some receiving individualized attention more than the others. Group discipleship creates peer accountability and de-emphasizes a hierarchical relationship; additionally, it also lessens the risk of forming co-dependent relationships.

That being said, one-on-one discipleship provides other benefits. It may feel less intimidating for a new believer to disciple one person than it does to start a group. It also can be helpful in certain situations to provide a greater level of investment, especially if the person shows strong spiritual hunger or is walking through intense pain.

Regardless of which approach you utilize, remember that structure exists to support the goal, which is making disciples. This is the emphasis. Structure should never replace the purpose.

Teach to Obey

When teaching on discipleship, I typically ask the class to list the four commands of the Great Commission. Almost inevitably, they describe the last as "teach them". It's an innocent mistake. But the implications are profound.

A massive gulf exists between the charge to "teach them" and the charge to "teach them to obey." One astute student remarked that this is similar to the difference between a teacher and a parent.

Dinnertime at my house often resembles a hostage negotiation. My wife and I dig deep within our arsenal of encouragement, exhortation, threats, and raw bribery for a single carrot. Victories seem pyrrhic at best. That being said, after four years of open warfare, I'm pleased to announce that one of our children now consumes a partially balanced diet. The jury is out on the others.

It's one thing for me to *teach* my kids the importance of eating a healthy diet. It's another entirely for me to actually *teach them to obey* eating their stupid vegetables. You get the point.

If my goal is to teach, then I will seek to broadly distribute my message. In our modern church age this includes sermons, seminars, podcasts, blogs, books, seminary, conferences, classes, and Sunday school, to name a few. All of these are wonderful – as long as we invest even more energy into *teaching to obey*.

If my goal is teaching to obey, my tactics must change entirely.

Mass distribution is impossible, no more plausible than mass parenting. Teaching to obey involves setting an example, self-discovery, and accountability. These all require time and life-on-life investment. As such, our discipleship model emphasizes the *process* of teaching to obey more than the *content*.

Content is important, obviously we don't want people applying the wrong things, but the *process* is generally the missing link for spiritual growth. Let's review a simple process for teaching to obey.

Friendship

Prior to a Lifegroup worship time to kick off the New Year, each member shared a way God changed his or her life through the group over the past twelve months. Many shared powerful stories but it was the last that most impacted me. I strained to hear as one woman quietly shared that it was through this group she learned to hear God.

It may seem mundane, but stories such as this describe the power of discipleship. Consider the massive implication for this woman's life! Learning to walk in ongoing relationship with God is foundational, it's life changing.

The group never taught on hearing God. This breakthrough occurred through the influence of other group members. She watched the example of others; she was encouraged – even challenged – through the relationships formed in the group. None of her change involved teaching, but instead it came through relationship. Your example matters far more than your words. This is why Jesus prioritized his twelve fishermen over the gathering crowds.

This reality is also frightening because it requires us to have a life worth modeling. My ability to make disciples is directly dependent on my willingness to first be a disciple. But don't disqualify yourself quite yet. No disciple is perfect. Sometimes the most powerful example is demonstrating how to respond when you fail. Seek to follow Jesus with everything and then, when you fail, model repentance.

Setting an example does not require any spiritual gift. You don't need to say anything. People will remember far more what you do than what you say.

Discovery

Learning the Bible is widely recognized as a critical component of discipleship in most churches, and rightfully so. However, it's not as easy as it seems. Simply telling new believers what to believe seldom bears lasting fruit. They might agree intellectually, but it is not until they discover the Word for themselves that they fully embrace the Truth on a heart level.

The recent experience of Antioch missionaries in the Arab world provides a clear example of this principle as two veteran missionaries unexpectedly found themselves in the midst of a historic move of God. They had ministered for years in their nation without seeing any lasting results. In fact, since the time of Mohammed there were no known movements of mass church-planting among Arab Muslims. But these men refused to give up and Jesus answered their prayers.

God sent them an unlikely man to catalyze this new movement. He was a former political activist who received Christ while watching an evangelistic TV show but had virtually no other spiritual growth. They committed to disciple him, but with the condition that he disciple others. He agreed and soon others joined the faith.

Within a year, hundreds of people gave their heart to Jesus and the church grew rapidly. The growth caused fundamental theological questions to emerge since all the leaders were new believers themselves. The missionaries resolved from the beginning to base everything in the Word of God. They chose to not answer the church leaders' questions but instead pointed them back to the Bible to discover the answers. Persecution is the reality of church-planting in the Middle East, and they recognized the importance of this emerging church being deeply grounded in the Word.

One morning a few months after the movement began, the missionaries walked into a meeting of the church leadership. They stepped inside the small room, blanketed in a haze of cigarette smoke, and noticed the men were passionately arguing a theological point. The missionaries listened on in confusion. As they tracked the argument, it suddenly dawned on them that these new believers were all heretics.

The sect of Islam to which these believers had previously adhered believed in reincarnation and they still held this belief. It was a shocking realization for these earnest missionaries as their goal of a church-planting movement teetered on the edge of instead morphing into a heretical sect. Not an ideal story for their newsletters back home.

Despite the deep concern they both felt, the missionaries still chose to not answer the question, and instead, pointed the Arab leaders to the Word of God. They sat aside, sweating nervously as the leaders debated the Scripture. After a lengthy and heated discussion, they finally announced their verdict: The Bible is clear that there is no reincarnation.

To our Bible-belt minds this seems shocking but to this culture the implications proved profound. This was a fundamental worldview native to this tribe; the word of a missionary is not powerful enough to reshape such a deeply held belief. But the Word of God is.

By patiently allowing the leaders to discover the Word for themselves, the missionaries created an environment to lay the deep foundations necessary for cultural change. Sure, they could have easily given the answer, but their word alone would never sustain the fortitude to transform a worldview.

This same dynamic applies to each of us. When we discover the Word for ourselves through the leadership of the Holy Spirit, the newly discovered truth provides a much deeper foundation for lasting change.

The discipleship material we provide at Antioch is meant to be delivered through a process of self-discovery. We utilize Discovery Bible Study as our basic structure. This tool is a series of questions that empower us to view the passage through a series of lenses. We start with five basic questions:

What is the main point of this passage?

What does it teach us about God?

What does it teach us about mankind and how we should live?

What do I need to apply to my life?

Who will I share this with?

We list passages of Scripture for various aspects of spiritual growth, be it spiritual seekers, new Christians, or maturing Christians seeking to grow in living Kingdom values. But the point of it all is self-discovery.

Accountability

"I have never experienced anything like this before!" exclaimed my friend. He recently joined our Lifegroup and the guys who met every other week for breakfast for discipleship. Vulnerable accountability is a core part of the group and other men had just finished discussing upcoming business travel. They sought sexual purity and, in response, shared temptations and corresponding boundaries such as unplugging the TV and avoiding the internet at night.

Though my friend previously attended a wide range of large and healthy churches, he had never experienced this type of openness. It's situations like this that serve as the ultimate distinction between teaching and teaching to obey. Discovery alone quickly descends into just a more effective form of teaching without the additional element of accountability.

We balk at the word "accountability." It may bring to mind past legalism or just feel constraining. But accountability is necessary for change. I've found that without accountability, I seldom fully respond to the leadership of God. I once sought to follow the words of Jesus in Matthew 6 by fasting entirely in secret. It went great until about

11am, at which point I began to question whether or not I heard God accurately. Maybe it was actually *next* Thursday. Maybe He meant *feasting* instead. Regardless, I ate a delicious lunch that day, simultaneously learning the valuable lesson that I need accountability to complete a fast.

Self-discovery is a powerful safeguard to protect accountability from growing legalistic. We don't hold people accountable to

WE DON'T HOLD PEOPLE ACCOUNTABLE TO OUR STANDARDS, BUT RATHER TO THE WORD OF GOD AND THE LEADERSHIP OF THE SPIRIT.

our standards, but rather to the Word of God and the leadership of the Spirit. There is certainly room to challenge each other, but ultimately everyone needs to hear God for themselves, and they need a community of people to hold them accountable to actually walk it out.

When in doubt, focus on these three elements of discipleship: build relationship, help people discover the Bible for themselves, and hold one another accountable to obey. It's not complicated, though difficult at times, but by committing to this process we will see incredible transformation.

THE CONTENT

Jesus charged us to teach them to obey *all that I have commanded you.* Oh, that's all? Easy. Seriously though, that seems a fairly impossible task. Getting people to obey anything in the Word is hard enough, but we're commissioned to include everything Jesus commanded us. We need to take a step back and realize that our responsibility in someone's discipleship process is limited. We're all on the road toward complete transformation into the image of Christ and all He commanded – but it is a journey. Our role in discipleship is to help the person take the next steps.

Great Commandment and Great Commission

Toward the end of Jesus' ministry, the Jewish religious leaders sought to undermine His authority by asking Jesus an impossible question: Which commandment is the greatest? The entire Old Testament described God's laws for His people and, absent the indwelling of the Holy Spirit, the people struggled to prioritize and apply them all. The question vexed religious leaders, yet in a few simple sentences Jesus cut through the confusion.

> 'Love the Lord your God with all your heart and with all your soul and with all your mind.' This is the first and greatest commandment. And the second is like it: 'Love your neighbor as yourself.' All the Law and the Prophets hang on these two commandments.
> Matthew 22:37-39

Love God and love people. That's the whole point of everything. Certainly unique situations create further complication and require clarity on how to obey these directives, but these summarize the commands of God. Add in the Great Commission, which is an extension of loving people, and you find three broad applications for the Church: Love God, Love Others, Love Those Who Don't Know Jesus. These three commands define Antioch's core values, as they do for many other churches around the world. In discipleship, "teaching to obey all that I commanded" points back to these three.

UP | IN | OUT

A simple approach to discipleship is challenging people to look Up, In, and Out.

UP: How are we growing in our relationship with God?

IN: How are we looking more like God in our character and relationships?

OUT: How are we fulfilling the Great Commission in our life?

Whether you are a mature believer or brand new Christian, this focus will lead to deeper growth in your relationship with Jesus.

I encourage discipleship group leaders to seek the Lord every few months for a fresh emphasis for their group. Try to think in terms of Up, In, and Out. Do you need to focus on one, or all three? Or a specific aspect of one, such as parenting, marriage, or purity?

Once you feel led to lead a certain direction, utilize the tools listed in this chapter to lead the group. Facilitate self-discovery in the Word surrounding the topic. Try to model ways to apply these truths; for example, if discussing prayer then set aside time to pray together. Share places of accountability each member feels necessary in response to the Word.

Don't be overwhelmed. On one level, if you start to consider everything people need in order to grow spiritually, then this process seems unbearable. But we need to keep perspective: The Holy Spirit is the One leading us into all truth. We cannot take over His job. Instead, we create an environment to help people respond to God's leadership. This is why we emphasize process over content. We have to trust God to lead us and we need each other to actually obey what He says.

If at some point you don't know what to do in a discipleship meeting, go back to the simplicity of Up, In, and Out by asking a basic accountability question for each. Something this basic leads to profound impact, as long as we don't give up.

New Believers

While I believe it's important to prioritize the process of discipleship over its content, the content still matters. This is especially true for new believers who don't yet know the Bible. A friend once described his spiritual journey to me and shared that after he committed his life to Jesus, he had no one to guide him in his new faith. All he knew to do was obey the Bible, so that's what he did with enormous zeal.

In principle, this seems wonderful. It's the main point of this whole book. However, in reality it was quite painful because no one ever told him to start in the New Testament. He spent a year seeking to conform to the Old Testament Law before finally realizing his mistake.

Each person is responsible before God for his or her own spiritual growth, but we, the Church, are charged to help new believers grow in the faith. Generally, I believe discipleship is not a cookie cutter process. Each person faces different challenges, so I've found discipleship should be tailored to address the pressing issues of life. This is why we encourage discipleship group leaders to seek the Lord for their group every few months.

However, I think discipleship requires a fairly linear process for new believers in order to build the right foundations. How can someone address purity if they don't yet understand sin? How do they learn to hear God's voice if they don't understand His character?

We still utilize the discovery process for new believers, but encourage disciple-makers to walk through a series of foundational discipleship lessons as the first step following salvation. We additionally provide lessons for people who are not yet believers and are seeking to explore faith. These pre-believer lessons point seekers to the character of God and eventually lead to a clear salvation message.

The Discipleship App

In order to deliver discipleship lessons and material described above, we created *The Discipleship App* available as a free download on iTunes and as a web app, accessible to any device. This is the official discipleship resource of Antioch Community Church and is available for any church to use as they'd like. We pray it is helpful, but also believe it is merely a tool to facilitate the processes and content outlined in this chapter.

The Discipleship App further clarifies Up, In, and Out by breaking them down into seven Kingdom values each. We provide Bible passages for each of these twenty-one values to use in a discovery process. Additionally, we share other resources, generally books or articles we have found helpful, and we also list group activities you can do together. Of course, God may lead you to do other things or your church may utilize a different resource, but we hope these serve as a starting point. You could easily spend a year on just one value or you could overview them all.

Technology is a wonderful thing, but remember you don't need it to make disciples. Jesus, Peter, Paul all did a great job with mostly illiterate people. All you need is the Word of God and the Holy Spirit. Our prayer is that technology supports, not supplants, the process of making disciples by teaching people to obey all that Jesus commanded us.

WHAT DISCIPLESHIP IS NOT

Anything powerful, when harnessed appropriately, provides an incredible potential for change. But it also creates an equal possibility of destruction if not utilized properly. The more powerful it is, the greater the potential for both transformation and devastation.

On April 26, 1986, the citizens of Pripyat, Ukraine experienced this firsthand. A decade earlier, a power plant was built on the outskirts of town with a promise of massive energy – both literal and economic. Over six hundred people were employed at the plant.

During a routine test, a sudden surge of power caused a fire and subsequent meltdown of the Chernobyl nuclear reactor. This crisis grew into the worst nuclear accident in history and led to the evacuation of the entire area. Humans cannot safely inhabit the abandoned city for another six hundred years.

Anything powerful requires safeguards, and discipleship is no different. We've described what discipleship is, but I find it equally important to describe what discipleship is not. History gives many examples of discipleship meltdowns, be it controlling models of ministry, overzealous legalism, or just plain weird practices. Unfortunately, each of these cause deep pain for those involved.

Let's be mindful of history and let's establish safeguards, but let's also avoid the temptation to let go of our Mission. Discipleship is powerful, and our world desperately needs spiritual power in order to see transformation. It's worth it to pursue, yet it's also important to stay wise in our application and specifically avoid three discipleship traps.

Personal Moses

"I'm so frustrated with discipleship!" my friend declared over lunch. I sat quietly, waiting for him to explain. "I feel like everyone wants me to be their personal Moses and I just can't take it anymore."

His righteous frustration put words to something I also felt. The goal of discipleship is to lead people to God. But often people want us to instead go to God on their behalf, which represents an Old Covenant mindset. Exodus 19-25 describes God demonstrating His power and laws to the Israelites on Mount Sinai, but only Moses was permitted to ascend the mountain. The rest of Israel remained at the base and waited for the man of God to return with the word.

This symbolizes one of the greatest dangers in discipleship: the tendency for us to try to become God's voice for those we serve, and for us to morph into a Personal Moses. After all, it's much easier to have Moses climb up the mountain while we stay in the comfort of our tents. And for us disciple-makers we easily derive warped significance by being someone else's Moses.

But by falling into this trap, we hinder the work of the Spirit. In John 16:7, Jesus tells us it is for our good that he is going away so that He can instead send the Helper. The Holy Spirit *within* is better for us than the privilege of living *alongside* the Incarnate Christ. I don't care how wise or how great a disciple-maker you are, the Spirit is better! Let's instead lead people up the mountain of God for themselves; let's teach them to hear God's voice on their own. Afterward, let's descend the mountain together and learn to actually live it in everyday life.

Practically, I almost never tell someone what to do. Instead of issuing commands, I try to help the people I disciple ask the right questions. For example, if someone asks what job offer they should take, I give them a few questions to pray through, such as: How does this fit with my calling? How will it affect my family? What are my motivations? I will give advice, but only after encouraging them to seek God for themselves and always with the disclaimer that this is their decision to make.

Counselors

"Where do you find time to do all these things?!" the class appeared to ask in unison. They sought to make disciples but felt my exhortation to model a Kingdom lifestyle, self-discovery, and accountability was impossible. I followed up, asking why this felt so challenging.

"We spend all of our time processing the previous week and discussing the latest personal issues. That alone takes 2 hours and we are burned out! Are you asking us to do more?" they testily retorted.

I paused, thinking through the familiar challenge, finally replying, "I believe that if you focus instead on building the right foundations, then there will be fewer problems to discuss."

This is the essence of the problem. People feel frustration and pain; furthermore, we live in a culture with deeply broken relational ties. The need for community is natural and it's not being met in modern society; this is why we do Lifegroup! But you need to be careful. It's not healthy for you to singlehandedly meet everyone's community needs; instead, the group as a whole should build strong relational ties.

The biggest problem hindering community is often the lack of spiritual foundations upon which a healthy life can be built. Address this first and everything else will fall into place.

Discipleship necessitates friendship, but this does not mandate you to develop into a counselor. I generally spend no more than a third to half of allotted discipleship time on catching up. I'm careful to never make it centered on me and to encourage group interaction during

> *DISCIPLESHIP NECESSITATES FRIENDSHIP, BUT THIS DOES NOT MANDATE YOU TO DEVELOP INTO A COUNSELOR.*

this time. However, I also strive to stay sensitive to the Spirit's leadership and will occasionally shift to focus on one person's needs.

Each group and each relationship comprise different dynamics. Some people require more prodding to speak openly, while others need a gentle exhortation to talk less in order to create space for others to share. Some groups I've led lead to relationships that end up becoming my closest friends; some groups have not progressed to the same level of friendship.

Don't feel the pressure to be everyone's best friend. You can't. Don't feel pressure to be ever-present and always available to provide counsel. That's why they have the Holy Spirit. And don't worry if you end up closer to some people than others. Jesus did the same.

In addition to the universal need for community, most people also experience places of deep pain – whether past or present. Community, including discipleship, should be a place of powerful healing. Often our mere presence itself is restorative; we will naturally share words of encouragement and sympathize from our own life journey. That being said, we should not try to usurp the role of biblically centered, professional counselors.

The line between discipleship and counseling often blurs together. When in doubt, encourage the person to seek out a godly counselor. For some people, they may only need one session, while for others it may grow into a critical component of their healing. Disciple-makers function similar to air traffic controllers. You don't need to provide everything for someone's spiritual life. Instead direct them where to go. At Antioch Waco, we provide a staff counselor to help diagnose and refer church members seeking help. If you church doesn't have a similar resource, consider building partnerships with Christian counselors in your city.

Force Feeders

Have you ever tried to force feed a child? Or anyone for that matter? I earlier shared the dietary wars fought in our household. As an ambitious pre-parent, I assumed feeding kids would be easy. Just stick the baby food in; they have to at least swallow it, right? I grossly underestimated the willpower newly budding in nine month olds. No matter how intensely I tried, each of my children successfully rebuffed my efforts and retaliated by ruining their clothing in the process.

Force feeding doesn't work spiritually any more than it does naturally. If people don't want it, then they won't take it. It's as simple as that. Jesus understood this truth; consider the people who did not end up becoming one of His disciples. Each contained a common denominator – they weren't spiritually hungry. Maybe they exhibited hunger to an extent, but not enough to sell everything like the Twelve.

Unfortunately, we cannot gauge spiritual hunger as accurately as Jesus, so avoid setting too high a bar. At the same time, the same principle still applies. We cannot help people who are not hungry.

The best way to avoid this is to set expectations at the beginning of a discipleship relationship. Try using the Matthew 7 parable of the two houses as vision, and share how this group will focus on applying the Word of God. It may be wise to agree together on expectations for attendance and for preparation. I generally encourage small discipleship groups or one-on-one relationships to have a set time limit of six months to one year, except for the general groups within each Lifegroup. You can always extend the time period if desired.

We all have bad days, so avoid casting judgment too quickly. But if you feel the group consistently shows no interest in responding for more than four to six months, then I recommend having a direct conversation to initiate change. Be clear but also be kind and understanding. Perhaps they are hungry, but your group isn't the best fit, or they have unique needs in this season of life. Start the conversation by restating the vision of the group, then share that you haven't sensed that the group members really wanted it. Ask them to pray about it for two weeks and then reinitiate with you if they would like to continue.

If they decline, don't take it personally. Remember that Jesus had discipleship opportunities fall through and had other disciples betray Him. Instead, use this as an opportunity to go find others who actually are hungry.

NEXT STEPS

As we conclude, let's remember Deana's story. A person was restored and is now restoring others. You may never preach, but you can disciple someone. You are charged to do this by Jesus Himself. Imagine the outcome if every single believer sought to fulfill our Commission. If we each simply discipled two to three people then entire societies would be transformed. And it all starts with one.

Before you read further, pause for a moment. Have you fully embraced this biblical mandate? Please take time to read back through the scriptures we've already discussed and consider all the implications. We need to re-program our perspective of what causes real spiritual growth. If we grasp the fullness of this calling then we will have power to press through both the boring and the difficult, and we will then walk into a move of God.

Discipleship Exercise

How has your understanding of biblical discipleship changed?

What most intimidates you in facilitating discipleship for others?

Who can you initiate with to start a new discipleship group?

What discipleship pitfalls do you most need to avoid?

Review The Discipleship App.

CHAPTER 5

Pastor Your Group

*Baptizing them in the name of the Father and of the
Son and of the Holy Spirit*

It's the phone call Lifegroup leaders dread. Incomprehensible sobs greet you on the other line while you patiently wait for your friend to blurt out, "My father just died."

It's the surprise coffee meeting with one of the men. What begins as a half-hearted admission of lust grows into a full-scale confession of adultery.

It's the group members who fear their son is clinically depressed, finally mustering up the courage to ask for advice.

No one feels equipped to deal with situations like these. Regardless of how many times you've received this call, sat through this meeting, or been asked for this counsel, these situations cause your stomach to drop. We grieve with our friends yet feel powerless to help. Sure, I can lead discussion and navigate awkward intro questions, but what do I tell someone who just experienced a miscarriage or was diagnosed with a terminal illness?

We live in a broken world. Destructive choices of loved ones, hidden sin, and health crises all pen the script to life's many tragedies. But Jesus loves to reverse the plot. He hijacks our suffering and turns it into a vehicle of grace.

The Example of Jesus

Consider the story of Lazarus. John 11:1-44 paints a painful scene. Mary and Martha cried out to Jesus to heal their dying brother, but He didn't arrive in time; their prayer for healing was unanswered. Jesus arrived three days later to a scene of grief. Mary poured out her pain when He stepped in the room, questioning God's lack of healing. Jesus never answered her questions; instead, He simply wept. Yet just a few verses later, Jesus stood in front of the tomb and commanded Lazarus to come out. The dead man rose to life and stepped out into the arms of his waiting family. The sisters asked for a miracle but endured a death. And then they witnessed a resurrection.

This story amazes me. Jesus knew Lazarus would rise, but still took time to grieve with Mary. It points to two powerful truths for believers: God draws close to us in our pain and He is always working a resurrection behind the scenes.

The example of Jesus should serve as a template for our response to the sufferings of others.

Presence is the best salve for pain. Don't try to give answers; often there aren't any. Instead, demonstrate a willingness to cry with the hurting and trust Jesus to bring life out of the darkness. Never forget we serve a God who defeated sin and death, even though we still live in the time of "now but not yet." His Kingdom power is accessible *now* to work freedom and healing, but the fullness of His reign is *not yet* revealed. Sin still holds sway over mankind and death still serves as the doorway into eternity, but underneath it all God brings His life.

The Comforter

In making disciples and leading a group, you will deal with others' sin – both the sinner and the victim. You will walk members through life's challenges. On your own this is a daunting task, but you are not alone. John 16:7 reveals the Holy Spirit to be our Comforter. This word literally describes "one who runs to the aide of the other." In verse 13, our advocate promises to guide us. The Holy Spirit runs to our aid and empowers us to comfort others no matter how deep the pain. Step out in faith to serve your group because ultimately it's not about you, but rather the Resurrector working through you.

"Baptizing Them"

The Great Commission commands us to baptize new believers in the name of the Father, Son, and the Holy Spirit. The act of baptism is a powerful illustration of the spiritual reality of new birth. It is an essential step in the discipleship process and a direct command from Jesus.

It also points to an important aspect of spiritual growth: the old aspects of worldly living and the corresponding hurt need to be washed away and replaced with a fresh knowledge of the character of God found in the Father, Son, and Spirit.

People will struggle to obey the commands of Jesus apart from this fullness of baptism into their new life. In addition to literal baptism, they need to grasp their new identity as a son or daughter of God, they need to truly understand the grace and mercy found in Jesus, and they need to be filled with the power of the Holy Spirit.

HELP

Consider the acronym HELP to describe the process for leaders and disciple-makers to respond to life's difficulties:

Have patience
Equip with the Word of God
Lead them into God's presence
Point them to professional support

When faced with challenges, utilize this template in order to determine your best response. Above all, remember the Comforter is with you, leading you into all things.

Have Patience

The word *process* is defined as a series of actions taken in order to achieve a particular end. A restoration or healing *process* will require time, otherwise it wouldn't be a *process*. When walking alongside someone, we often feel we know the solution to his or her problem. Our formula seems infallible:

If they would just stop_____ or just believe _____ or just do _____ then their sin/grief/pain/troubles would go away!

Unfortunately, life doesn't work this way. The formula doesn't work for your life, so stop deceiving yourself into thinking it will for someone else.

Sinless God is patient with our *process*; as sinful man surely we ought to extend the same for one another. Two of the most potent tools we wield in the healing process are byproducts of patience: **listening** and **presence**.

Anyone can use these, yet few actually do. Don't try to rush someone's process by giving pat answers, even if they are true. Take time to listen as they pour out their pain; and when words fail, simply be present. The time may come for action and speaking truth, especially if the problem is sin, but start with patience, and you might discover your quick solution isn't quite as accurate.

Equip with the Word of God

It's an increasingly common scenario: A new couple attends the group for a month and shows signs of deep spiritual hunger, but after a casual discussion one evening after Lifegroup, it dawns on you that they're living together outside of marriage. To compound the problem, they have a child already and don't seem to realize anything is amiss. How do you respond?

More and more our society attempts to blur the lines of sin. People are still spiritually hungry, but hunger is no indication people actually know the Word of God. We feel insecure bringing it up, after all they are doing their best and things seem to be going ok. What's the big deal?

In moments like these, I find it's important to remember the truth that **sin always brings death**, even to the ignorant. We cannot claim to love people and yet sit idly by while destruction spreads through their lives.

Develop the habit of pointing your group to the Word of God for answers. Let them discover the Word of God and the corresponding conviction of the Holy Spirit. At times this may even require a rebuke. I hate doing this, but recognize it's one of the purest acts of love. When you give a gift, you receive the joy of the response.

> *DEVELOP THE HABIT OF POINTING YOUR GROUP TO THE WORD OF GOD FOR ANSWERS.*

When you share an encouragement, the recipient often reciprocates. But when you challenge someone, you risk a misunderstanding – even the relationship itself – in order to express concern. You risk everything and possibly gain nothing, all for someone else's sake.

Lead Them into God's Presence

Wes walked up to me after a church service and asked for prayer. His sister died only a few days earlier and she was the stable pillar in his family. For decades, he lived bound by drug addiction. Her life had been his only light. He knew she had prayed daily for his freedom and, in his grief, he felt the best way to honor her memory was to seek prayer for deliverance.

He stood timidly and poured out his story through tears. Together we cried out for a touch from God. Instantly, Wes was healed. Years of addiction were broken off in a moment. Wes still required a deep healing process in his life, but the power of God was the catalyst for his freedom.

We tend to swing like a pendulum when seeking freedom and healing. We swing from believing the solution to everything is empathetic processing, to believing the solution always lies in professional help, to believing the only answer is a supernatural touch. Generally, the solution is all three. I'm deeply grateful for the capable hands of doctors, but also believe we must still cry out for healing. I believe counselors and medicine are important aspects of treating mental illness. And I also believe in a God who leads us out of darkness.

The role of disciple-makers and Lifegroup leaders is to lead our groups to the presence of God while also pointing them to professionals trained to bring skillful care. Most personal testimonies demonstrate the importance of both while navigating the path to healing.

Included as part of *The Discipleship App*, we recommend *Tending Your Heart*[1] and *The Steps to Freedom*[2] as resources for disciple-makers and Lifegroup leaders. *Tending Your Heart* is a guide to help individuals process with the Lord the instinctive lies they believe. Many have found tremendous breakthrough as they develop a lifestyle of allowing God to speak into places of pain. It is not a one-time experience, but rather a consistent conversation with the Spirit.

The Steps to Freedom in Christ by Neil T. Anderson facilitates a process of revealing past (and present) places of sin, unforgiveness, fear, and negative spiritual experiences the enemy uses to exploit an individual's life. The tool guides the person through a process of renouncing sin and receiving the freedom of God in its place.

I hope every discipleship relationship creates space to walk through these valuable tools as part of the journey into encountering God.

Point Them to Professional Support

When teaching a child to swim, it's important for them to understand what depths they can and can't handle. Over time they may develop the skill to venture out alone into deep waters, but what matters right now is what they can do today.

Likewise, most leaders will at times find themselves out of their depth. Don't be discouraged; instead, know where to get support. As stated earlier, we provide a licensed counselor at Antioch Waco who is equipped to evaluate and refer to outside support. In cases of suspected mental illness, such as depression, eating disorders, or addiction, we want our leaders to seek professionals rather than take it on themselves. The group will still play a vital supporting role, but should not try to supplant the role of a counselor.

I believe certain marital crises or situations of financial indebtedness are best helped through a trained counselor, in addition to the accountability within the group. A general rule is *when in doubt, ask.* One important note: many times a person's healing journey will require medication for both physical and mental illness. Leaders should never recommend someone to stop taking their prescription. If the person is planning to stop, ask them to talk to their doctor before making a decision. If you feel the counseling experience isn't helping the individual, then reach out to another counselor for a second opinion.

These difficulties remind us that life is challenging and pain is complicated, but in the process we must remember God is always seeking to resurrect us into fresh life.

YOUR RESPONSIBILITIES

As we support people on their path to healing and breakthrough, we all have a few responsibilities. These are necessary safeguards to help others find restoration.

Duty to Report

In certain situations, group members may confide troubling information that requires immediate action. These are suicidal thoughts, homicide, and abuse of a minor – both past and present. You have a legal duty to report, but more importantly, it's the right thing to do. We never want to risk someone hurting themselves or others while we waited.

If someone expresses suicidal thoughts you should always take it seriously. If in doubt, ask them directly if they are considering suicide. If you feel they are at risk, call 911 immediately. Seek professional help as quickly as possible.

You must also report any allegation of child abuse; for those in Texas, do this at **txabusehotline.org** or **1-800-252-5400**, or research the requirements for your home state. This holds true regardless of whether you've heard from the victim or the perpetrator. If the abuse happened in the past, even decades before, and the abuser is still around children, you still must report.

After you've reported the situation, reach out to a counselor or pastor for help navigating the next steps, but only after you have first contacted the relevant authorities.

Confidentiality

Professional therapists are sworn to confidentiality. Without it, patients may feel reluctant to truly share their heart. While Lifegroup leaders and disciple-makers are not legally bound by these same requirements, the principle still holds true. Breaching trust causes deep pain.

Most leaders would never do this intentionally, but it can still accidentally leak out. If you feel the need to tell someone else something that was shared with you in confidence, and sometimes you will, then tell the person first. If you need support on how to address a problem, don't share the person's name when seeking advice from a pastor or mentor.

The duty to report listed above always trumps confidentiality. Other situations may also require you to share with someone. But let's strive to honor in every possible way.

NEXT STEPS

This chapter just briefly addressed the range of challenges in people's lives; the problem is compounded by the uniqueness of each person's situation. We recognize this chapter contains heavy topics. Sharing Lifegroup bloopers stories is much more enjoyable than confronting the sobriety of people's problems amidst a broken world. As we conclude the chapter, let's return to the story of Lazarus. Jesus weeps with us in our pain and works resurrection in our destruction.

Before you move on, pause for a moment and consider a powerful testimony you've recently heard. Try to recall the specifics. Most great redemption stories began with one of the challenges listed in this chapter. Someone experienced sin, pain, or death. And God transformed their pain into a place of grace. You may need to walk alongside a friend through a challenging situation, but this may also be a front row seat to a dynamic story of redemption. In the end, you'll find it's worth it.

Pastoral Questions

What past experience do you have providing pastoral care for people walking through difficult situations? How did you respond?

What common scenarios do you anticipate experiencing? How would you respond?

What intimidates you about walking alongside others in this way?

Pray for one another to walk in confidence and the wisdom of the Holy Spirit.

CHAPTER 6

Facilitate Your Group

I walked into the room filled with faith. My second night to ever lead a Lifegroup seemed promising as I watched several guests arrive, including a man I'd just met the night before. It felt like a move of God waiting to happen. That is, right up until the discussion time.

I asked the group to describe their relationship with their father. The question was meant to lead us into discussing our heavenly Father. Several members shared vulnerably and then I noticed my new friend raise his hand.

"May I read something?" he asked, holding his Bible.

"Of course!" I replied, excited that after a mere hour into this new group we already stood on the cusp of spiritual depth.

His choice of passage was a surprise. To be honest, I expected the Prodigal Son, not a judgment passage from Isaiah, but he seemed confident and I eagerly awaited the explanation. And waited … and continued to wait. He proceeded to read several long chapters in a painfully slow, monotone voice. After ten minutes he abruptly stopped without explanation or summary. Nothing. My friend attempted to bail out the hopelessly derailed discussion by linking the passage to the topic but his feeble bid fell on deaf ears. None of the guests ever returned.

Several days later, I met with the man to clarify the vision for Lifegroup, politely explaining that we try to limit our talking in order to provide everyone a chance to share. He wholeheartedly agreed and then proceeded to tell me stories of the angels he speaks with regularly. I grew even more alarmed.

I felt apprehension build the following week as Tuesday night neared but experienced a deep relief when he never arrived. Lifegroup was great and hope rekindled.

The following week wasn't as fortunate. I was dismayed to see his car pull up, and raced to meet him outside in order to respectfully remind him to stick to short scriptures or summarize if he wants to read a passage. He kindly agreed and assured me it was no problem. The night began on uncomfortable footing. Several guests obliviously walked through the door while the core members shared a knowing look. Our new member attempted to correct another member as she shared a testimony but after the brief mishap, the rest of the meeting flowed smoothly. Until the discussion.

I watched him open the Bible after the first question, feeling slightly guilty for the knot forming in my stomach at the sight of God's Word. His hand shot up.

"Can I share a word?" he assertively asked, with an innocent expression on his face.

"Is it long?" I replied, oozing awkwardness.

"A few chapters" he countered. I was amazed. How on earth did he forget not one, but two direct conversations related to this very thing?

"Can you please either summarize or pick a few verses in order to give others a chance to share?" I responded, hoping to remind him of our previous dialogue.

"HOW ON EARTH CAN YOU SUMMARIZE THE WORD OF GOD?!" He loudly declared in state of righteous indignation. The members hid their smiles while the guests looked on in horror.

"I'm sure you can figure it out," I replied, well past the point of seeking to salvage the group.

In the ensuing silence, he eventually blurted out John 11:35, "Jesus wept" and never spoke again. None of the guests ever returned, nor did my new antagonist. Through the experience, I learned Lifegroup doesn't always go as planned.

Unfortunately, we can't spare you every awkward situation. Every leader has a collection of war stories such as mine. It's going to happen, don't sweat it and move on. But we do believe we can give you a head start and empower you to avoid many of the pitfalls found in facilitating a group.

This chapter will walk you through the various elements of leading a Lifegroup meeting: fellowship, intro question, worship, vision, discussion, ministry time, kids, and administration. Each section will provide a general list of best practices, plus a few ways to take this aspect of Lifegroup to the next level. We'll also share a few things to always avoid. Finally, we will list a few common models for the best ways to structure your meeting.

True, things will occasionally be uncomfortable, but we pray you will both feel equipped and have grace to laugh in the midst of it.

FELLOWSHIP

"Ed, can you bring drinks?" asked the young adult Lifegroup leader, who sought to integrate the new member into the group by pulling him into the preparation process for a Lifegroup dinner.

Ed loved to serve; this responsibility excited him by giving the chance to reciprocate for all the ways others cared for him in his journey of faith.

He arrived promptly with several ice chests in tow. The first cooler contained ice-cold tea and lemonade. The second contained individual bottles of Jack Daniels punch. The third was filled to the brim with beer. Ed gave extravagantly by buying enough alcohol for a college fraternity, beaming with innocent pride at the chance to help. The leaders felt something else entirely as their Lifegroup appeared at risk of disintegrating into a keg party.

Creating a warm environment of fellowship is the second most important part of the night, and it doesn't always go according to plan.

Best Practices

The desire for authentic community is universal, especially in an increasingly disconnected world. God designed us to need one another. Lifegroup exists to help meet this critical need. The goal for Lifegroup extends beyond community as ultimately we strive for discipleship. But we must recognize people will never embrace discipleship without first experiencing real community.

True community spreads far beyond the weekly meeting, but the Lifegroup meeting functions as a platform to build relationships. This is especially true of those with busy lives, as these two hours may be their only social activity for the week.

To establish a healthy community, you need to acknowledge the importance of fellowship time. I generally set aside twenty to thirty minutes to informally talk and connect. To achieve this, bring great snacks – not your stale Doritos and off-brand soda – and consider ways to set up the room to maximize interaction.

FELLOWSHIP

DO

// Bring great snacks
// Create a hospitable environment
// Set aside 20-30 minutes

DON'T

// Let cliques form
// Neglect guests

If you want to take it to the next level, consider hosting Lifegroup dinner periodically, with each member contributing part of the meal (one warning: this may become a burden if done too frequently). To grow even further, take a Lifegroup retreat or go on a mission trip together.

Ultimately, church is people. Relationships, not structure, are the primary building blocks of the Kingdom. These seemingly insignificant times serve an eternal purpose.

Things to Avoid

Setting aside the well-recognized danger of bad snacks, avoid the pitfall of allowing cliques to form. It's unavoidable that people will connect better with some than with others. That's life. But the leaders should pay attention to people who don't seem as connected, either because they are shy or because they are new, and find ways to help them integrate with the group.

INTRO QUESTION

I selected the perfect question to start off Lifegroup; it was a light-hearted attempt at self-deprecatory humor, which I hoped would cause people to feel comfortable together.

"Describe your funniest run-in with the police." I asked, anticipating stories of comical misunderstandings. Somehow, I grossly underestimated the depravity of my group.

The conversation took a negative turn with the second story as a member shared, in vivid detail, a wild night of partying, out-running the police into a forest, and hiding in trees. Other less-sanctified members cheered him on with similar stories of evading arrest and general criminality. After a forty-five-minute-long celebration of crime, I lamely sought to lead the group into worship.

The purpose of an intro question is to facilitate conversation amongst the group in order to get to know one another. Fails notwithstanding, it is a great way to engage guests and to help people feel at ease talking together.

Best Practices

Intro question(s) should be limited in scope. Don't ask open-ended questions unless you're prepared to devote a significant portion of the night to the topic. When possible, tie the question to the discussion theme. For example, if discussing parenting, ask, "What traditions from your family will you pass on to your children?"

Seek variety between fun and deep with the questions. One week ask about everyone's favorite summer activity. The next week inquire about fresh revelation of God's character from each member. Consider alternating group members to share more in depth in order to learn more about one another.

INTRO QUESTION

DO

// Alternate between fun and deep
// Share names weekly
// Link to the discussion topic

DON'T

// Say "ice-breaker"
// Ask questions which isolate members

Remember to share names and basic biographic information consistently. Newer members may especially struggle with feeling like an outsider if leaders mistakenly assume everyone knows each other.

To take this aspect of the group to the next level, consider a group game or activity.

Things to Avoid

While these questions serve to foster relational depth, as the first story demonstrates, intro questions can backfire. Avoid ever saying the word "ice-breaker," instead cast vision for getting to know one another to start off the group.

Evaluate how members may perceive questions and avoid discussions that may isolate. For example, in a group with singles, don't ask about everyone's honeymoon destination.

If you lead long enough, you'll inevitably experience uncomfortable conversations. Just press on, the group will survive.

VISION

My friend embarked on the exciting journey of leading a new group. He attended my Lifegroup for years and we determined it was time to branch out. He was thrilled when several men joined his new group and, following my leadership, initiated discipleship.

I repeatedly stressed the importance of clear vision, and my mentoring paid off. He took the lesson to heart and kicked off his new group with vision. I was pleased. Until I heard what he said.

"How'd it go?" I asked him after their first meeting.

"Well, I did what you said. But I'm not sure it worked," he sheepishly replied.

Slight alarm raced through my mind. I raised my eyebrows, "What happened?"

"I froze and forgot what to say," he responded. "So I explained that Jesus had 12 disciples and so I, too will make disciples. These men would now be mine. I clarified that I'm their discipler and they will my disciplees."

I buried my head in my hands, not sure whether to laugh or cry. Vision plays an important role in the context of group life. It serves as the catalyst to communicate purpose and direction. Without it, the group regresses into a monotonous routine and eventually declines. It's not enough to have a vision; you must also regularly communicate it.

Best Practices

"Vision leaks" states Bill Hybels[3], a well-known pastor and leadership coach. He drew the illustration of a bucket, filled with water but also poked through with holes at the bottom. The holes represent life's struggles – bills, work stress, kids' activities, relational strain – to name a few. Casting vision fills the bucket, but immediately after the words leave your mouth, the vision begins to leak. The only solution is to repeatedly fill the bucket.

Never take for granted that people understand the purpose of your group. Some care about community, others consider it a Bible study, and still others only come to find a date or because their spouse is pressuring them. Vision statements alone won't solve these problems, but they will help.

Identify a few fundamental Bible verses for your group. I've typically used Acts 2:42-47 or Matthew 28:18-20. Read the verse and share key attributes as ideals for your Lifegroup.

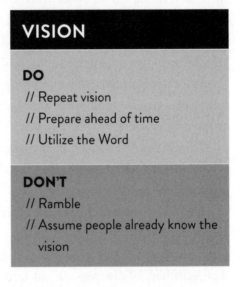

VISION

DO

// Repeat vision

// Prepare ahead of time

// Utilize the Word

DON'T

// Ramble

// Assume people already know the vision

For example, describe the depth of community found in Acts and the persistent feeling of awe in worship. Communicate the clarity of purpose in the Great Commission and cast vision for where your group is called to "Go." Consider facilitating a Discovery Bible Study on these passages one week for discussion.

The UP | IN | OUT discipleship template described in Chapter 4 is an effective way to cast Lifegroup vision. Challenge the group to "Look Up, In, and Out." Our ambition is to encounter God (Look Up), love one another (Look In), and love those who don't know Jesus (Look Out). One year I even created corresponding hand motions. Cheesy? Yes – but effective.

To take vision to the next level, ask group members to share a story of how their life was impacted by an aspect of Lifegroup vision.

Things to Avoid

A general rule for communication: people only remember one thing you say. Avoid the mistaken assumption that the more you talk, the more powerful the vision. Often the opposite is true; a rambling vision will prove ineffective. I encourage all new leaders to write out their vision statement in advance. Even practice it. Over time it'll feel second nature if you will invest in the skill of casting vision.

WORSHIP

It was my week to watch kids; however, to help my co-leaders, I offered to create a worship playlist for the adults. Christmas was rapidly approaching so I included a worshipful carol. Or so I thought.

In my haste to prepare, I neglected to actually listen to the songs I'd selected. I planned to play "O Holy Night" but instead choose "Silent Night," sung by a children's choir. I realized my mistake when I heard the gentle tune of the revered lullaby from the room next door.

By the time I recognized the error, the song was half-finished, too far along to change. I half-cringed/half-laughed for the next two minutes as the adults attempted to sing along.

The goal of worship is to encounter God. Fortunately for us, His presence is already with us no matter how awkward of an environment we create.

Best Practices

Try to start the worship time with a call to worship. People attend the group because they want God, but we all live distracted lives. Before hitting "play", seek God for a way to pull the groups' attention away from the mundane challenges of life and onto the person of Jesus.

Declare praises of thankfulness, speak out the attributes of God, take a moment to still your heart to listen to God's voice, read a Psalm in unison. These and more empower us to focus on our King.

Practically, select songs familiar to the members so they can participate. Consider building a Lifegroup playlist of ten to twelve songs you regularly sing. Be careful introducing new songs; new worship is essential to keep the time fresh, but don't do more than one new song in a meeting.

Some groups utilize YouTube worship videos with lyrics to help members engage. Generally, two to four songs works best in a standard Lifegroup, though leave plenty of room for God to lead otherwise. If possible, keep songs in the same key. If you don't know what that means, then don't worry about it.

While you worship, also seek to create an atmosphere of ministry. Read 1 Corinthians 14:26 or Colossians 3:16 in order to remind your group that God gives everyone something to bring. Encourage members to pray for each other during worship and lead out by example.

WORSHIP

DO

// Create a bank of 10-12 songs

// Introduce new songs one at a time

// Create space for ministry to each other

DON'T

// Play lengthy/dancing/prophetic songs

// Forget to explain experience to guests

Consider adding depth by facilitating the Lord's Supper as a group or by leading an extended time of intercession for the needs of individuals within the group or the world around us.

Take worship to the next level by hosting Lifegroup worship nights. There is a depth of worship that often requires extended time in the presence of God. We've periodically hired babysitters in order to create this type of longer, undistracted environment.

Things to Avoid

Many songs which are powerful in personal devotional times or large services are awkward when sung in a Lifegroup, these include long prophetic songs, high energy "dancing" music, lengthy instrumental interludes, and vocalists with a supernaturally high vocal range. There isn't anything wrong with these songs; it's just uncomfortable to try to sing with eight adults in a small room.

Also, stay mindful of any new guest's experience. You may feel comfortable with demonstrative charismatic expressions, but does this distract them from encountering God? 1 Corinthians 14:1-25 challenges us to consider our brothers and sisters in our worship.

Lifegroup is a wonderful place to both learn and express spiritual gifts; please don't hold back from passionately seeking God! At the same time, strive to make the experience approachable for new members by taking time to calmly and biblically explain what occurs. We want encounters with God to be translated so that old and new members alike can encounter Jesus.

DISCUSSION

The discussion time typically produces the most anxiety in leaders, often for good reason.

A Lifegroup member seemed to miss normal social cues. She regularly interrupted other members while they shared and tended to answer each question multiple times.

Each week, I increasingly dreaded the discussion until it became unbearable. My wife initiated with the member and was forced to clarify "talking rules" – no interrupting and only answering one time per question to leave time for others to share. Fortunately, she responded well.

While it's true there is a potential for uncomfortable moments, discussion is far more frequently a powerful time. The goal is to simply get people into God's Word. Most people live surrounded by the latest teaching – be it podcasts, conferences, books or sermons – but rarely are we led to discover the Bible for ourselves.

Best Practices

At Antioch Waco, we utilize Discovery Bible Study, the same process we use in discipleship groups, as the basis for our Lifegroup discussions. This process encourages people to look at a particular passage of Scripture through different lenses by asking questions. These questions generally don't vary much week-to-week. The goal is a reproducible process that trains people to discover the Bible for themselves and to learn to apply it to their lives.

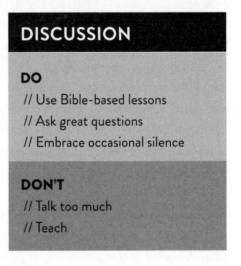

DISCUSSION

DO

// Use Bible-based lessons

// Ask great questions

// Embrace occasional silence

DON'T

// Talk too much

// Teach

Asking questions is the requisite skill for great discussions. The best leaders talk the least; rather than imparting more information, they ask questions to draw out others. As a result, silence is a normal part of a discussion. Don't worry about these pauses, often this is a sign people are thinking and extra space will give introverts an opportunity to mentally process.

At the end, leave time to wait on the Lord for each member to consider how they need to apply the passage to his or her life. Share with each other during the ministry time or the discipleship group and then remember to check-in the following week.

Take discussion to the next level by sending the passage (or topic) and the corresponding questions to the group members prior to the meeting. This provides an opportunity for them to wrestle with the Scripture first and then arrive with both revelation and questions for the group.

Things to Avoid

Notice this time is titled "discussion", not "teaching". This is intentional. The body of Christ is blessed through the gift of teaching, but I don't believe Lifegroup is the best venue for this expression. Occasionally, leaders may feel that a topic requires it. This is fine, but should not become the standard for the group. I recommend leaders contact their pastor if they plan to teach regularly.

God speaks to each member of the group, and a safe community is a wonderful place to learn to discover the Bible and hear the voice of God. Great discussions provide an avenue for this discipleship.

MINISTRY TIME

Time froze as the mob rushed past. I stretched out my arm in vain to stop the unfolding catastrophe, but moved far too slowly. Moments later, I grimaced as surprised screams erupted from the room next door. My removal from leadership appeared inevitable.

The Lifegroup met in the duplex of a reluctant member. Several other guys lived in the apartment and their fraternity brothers lived next door. Some of them periodically attended and were friends with a few of the ladies in the group. Following discussion, the Lifegroup routinely split into smaller groups for ministry, with the men going to one room and the women to another. The guys generally finished after a few minutes while the women regularly prayed for nearly an hour.

On this particular night, forty-five minutes after the group officially ended, a neighbor walked over wearing only a towel, completely oblivious to the ladies in the nearby room. His friends recognized an opportunity, promptly removed the towel and threw the unwitting naked man into the room of praying women.

I've never seen a man run away that quickly. Fortunately, the women claim to have only seen a white blur fleeing the room.

Ministry time is the most important part of the night. It's the best environment for people to share their hearts, a great opportunity for accountability, and often the place for salvation. It's also the occasional scene of a disaster.

Best Practices

Plan to leave at least ten minutes for ministry. We've generally found it most effective to break into same gender groups of no more than 2-3 people. Leaders should use this time to connect with new guests. Pay attention to the prompting of the Spirit, because often He will lead you to ask a question to open someone's heart.

MINISTRY TIME

DO

// Model vulnerability

// Share the Gospel if in doubt

// Follow up throughout the week

DON'T

// Run out of time

// Neglect guests

Encourage people to share vulnerably by leading out by example. Share places you'd like to apply the Word and create an environment of grace-filled accountability. Always end by praying for each person.

Take ministry time to the next level by writing down specific prayer points and texting encouragements to members during the week. Follow up on the issue after the next meeting to check in on progress and breakthrough.

Things to Avoid

The greatest hindrance to ministry is the tendency for groups to run out of time. Generally, unless leaders plan ahead, other elements of the group will go longer than anticipated and the ministry time will be forgotten.

This time is fundamentally important if discipleship is our goal. A discussion may impart knowledge, even self-discovery, but foundations are not laid until knowledge grows into application.

KIDS

Lifegroup with kids is always an adventure. The adults were in the middle of a much-needed ministry time when a sudden shout interrupted the rare calm. "We are going to get our BB guns!" the boys yelled as they raced past the dads sitting peacefully on the porch. Twenty-five children of various ages attended the group on this warm summer evening. The men were tired, mainly because of the small tribe of their progeny gathered next door, and elected to continue on with praying together before investigating.

Minutes later a loud BOOM shook the porch; the young boys quickly emerged and proudly displayed the freshly decapitated Copperhead snake. Their valiant effort to protect the girls with BB guns failed, but the neighbor showed up and his shotgun blast proved plenty capable.

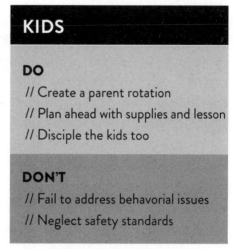

KIDS

DO
// Create a parent rotation
// Plan ahead with supplies and lesson
// Disciple the kids too

DON'T
// Fail to address behavorial issues
// Neglect safety standards

The moms inside were justifiably alarmed – both by the snake and their husbands' indifference. But seriously, with twenty-five kids what else can you expect?

In my conversations with leaders over the years, they are most vexed by the dilemma of kids in Lifegroup. Many experienced dynamic groups as students and young adults but cannot seem to find the same life in family Lifegroup.

To be sure, kids change everything. But Lifegroup should be just as powerful an experience for children as it is adults. This requires significantly more work, but also provides a significantly greater reward.

The goal of kids in Lifegroup is the same as adults: *Discipleship*.

Best Practices
Discipleship requires intentionality, both for adults and children. I suggest finding or developing a kids Lifegroup discussion guide for

use each week. My church sends one out alongside the guide for adults.

Most groups set up a rotation of adults to watch over the kids. To maximize this method, appoint a member in charge of preparing the necessary materials and communicating the discipleship plan to the kids' workers each week. Create a basket for kids' supplies to have on hand and commit to a regular rhythm of teaching kids' lessons. Some groups may choose to pay babysitters. This approach is also fine, just ensure it's affordable for every member and still leads to discipleship, not just babysitting.

In order to protect children, the policy at Antioch Waco requires a minimum of two adults to watch over the kids. No adult should be alone with a child who is not his or her own, and, as an added precaution, all of our Lifegroup leaders are asked to undergo a background check. This may seem obtrusive, but we believe the safety of our children is well worth it. I recommend other churches adopt a similar standard.

To take kids' discipleship to the next level, try to integrate them with the adult Lifegroup. We believe it's powerful for children to see their parents worship. To achieve this, play kid friendly songs and find ways to include activities during discussion. Remember, kids need vision too! Find creative ways to communicate the purpose of each element in the group and then lead them along with their parents.

Things to Avoid

In addition to child safety protocols, always remember to check in on the experience. Debrief the night with the people assigned to children each week and look for trends. Are there particular behavioral challenges with a child? Do you notice consistent values differences between children? None of these are fun to address, but if you discover recurring themes, you need to discuss it with their respective parents.

This is part of the challenge of Lifegroup but also the power of the group. Lifegroup allows us to get a close look into one another's lives, and we cannot hide. This leads to tension, but often that tension is necessary for a subsequent transformation.

ADMINISTRATION

The word administration scares people, and rightfully so in many situations. However, Lifegroup administration need not be overwhelming. The overall goal is to distribute group responsibilities so no one person bears the entire burden.

Best Practices

Each group should establish a sign-up sheet in order to rotate as many responsibilities as possible: kids, host home, and snacks generally serve as the top three. Planning six to eight weeks at a time seems to be a good rhythm for most groups. You can utilize paper and pen or any number of online calendars.

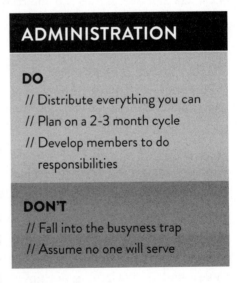

If you want to take administration to the next level, consider distributing responsibility for every aspect of the group, including all the aspects of the Lifegroup meeting. This will require time spent training and giving feedback, particularly with discussion and worship, but the effort will bear fruit by both developing new Lifegroup leaders and also removing pressure off of the current leaders.

ADMINISTRATION

DO
// Distribute everything you can
// Plan on a 2-3 month cycle
// Develop members to do responsibilities

DON'T
// Fall into the busyness trap
// Assume no one will serve

Things to Avoid

The main pitfall with administration is simply not doing anything.

We easily fall into the busyness trap. We feel too busy to plan ahead, which in turn, creates more work in the future. It quickly develops into a cycle. The busier you feel, the more important it is to effectively plan.

Avoid the mistaken assumption that people are unwilling to serve. I've found people desire to contribute, but are waiting to be asked. You may feel overwhelmed by the group consistently meeting in your home, but unless you ask for other hosts, the situation will not change.

If after your best efforts, still no one is willing to share the load, consider meeting with individual members to encourage participation. If this still doesn't produce change, talk to your pastor and consider launching a new group. The lack of engagement might indicate the need for fresh vision for everyone involved. Help the existing members find new groups and launch out with a new focus.

GROUP MODELS

Many leaders find it difficult to establish a convenient group structure. Travel distance, extra-curricular activities, homework, night shifts, and bedtimes all hinder the process of developing a functional group rhythm.

I've found a right perspective to be essential toward navigating these difficulties: *no matter the issue, there is **always** a solution*. I've coached leaders in dozens of cities across America, representing a wide variety of seasons of life. You may need to completely reinvent Lifegroup in order to express Kingdom values, but there is always a way. With this in mind, the chart below highlights three models we've found most helpful. Your church may create additional models. If you don't already have a plan, I suggest you start by utilizing one of the approaches listed and then adapt accordingly until you find something that works.

MODEL 1 | STANDARD

OVERVIEW

Weekly Lifegroup meetings plus a separate weekly or every other week men's and women's discipleship group.

Works best for: People who live in geographic proximity, groups with no kids, groups with preschool or younger kids.

Pros

- Creates multiple connection points if people frequently miss the group
- Provides solid discipleship opportunities by facilitating a focused meeting

Cons

- Adds travel time to the multiple meetings especially if people live far away
- Creates extra coordinating and scheduling responsibilities for the multiple meetings

MODEL 2 | ALL-IN-ONE

OVERVIEW

Weekly meetings, combining the full Lifegroup meeting together with men's and women's discipleship.

Works best for: Families with school-age children, people with busy work schedules, people who live far apart.

Pros

- Accomplishes everything in one evening per week, ensuring access to discipleship for the whole group.
- Connect consistently by meeting weekly

Cons

- Necessitates a lengthier meeting to accomplish everything
- Causes kids to get tired or rowdy due to the longer meeting

MODEL 3 | ROTATION

OVERVIEW

Varied meeting focused; twice per month Lifegroup; twice per month men's and women's discipleship groups.

Works best for: Busy families, people with long-term Lifegroup and ministry involvement who need a break.

Pros

• Provides a model for busy people

• Allows for a more low-key experience for people needing a break, without getting isolated.

Cons

• Creates a challenge to maintain consistency

• Difficult to build community with new members or less-discipled people

• Leads to disconnection if people regularly miss

WIND AND SAILS

Lifegroup is similar to sailing a large ship. The seaworthiness of the ship, the size of the sails, and the strength of the masts each factor into how far the ship will go. However, the most critical quality cannot be controlled … the wind. Without the wind, the sailing ship isn't going anywhere, regardless of the quality of its sails.

In the same way, Lifegroup, no matter how well led, will not grow full of "life" without the Holy Spirit. Diligently work to strengthen your group. Devote energy into learning the skill of leadership. Don't allow yourself to be overwhelmed by this chapter. No one is perfect. Above all remember that more than anything, we need a move of God.

Lifegroup Questions

What are the three biggest strengths of your current group? What are the three main challenges?

Where do you experience the most stress in facilitating Lifegroup?

If you have never led before, which aspect of facilitating a group is most intimidating? What can you do to prepare and build confidence?

What stood out to you most from this chapter regarding each aspect of the Lifegroup night?

What three changes do you need to make now?

CHAPTER 7

Multiply Your Group

March, 2010

The humid air smothered my face as I stepped out of the airport terminal in Port-au-Prince, Haiti. The situation inside the arrivals lounge seemed to teeter on the edge of chaos; baggage haphazardly distributed by a bare bones airport staff working alongside a nearly non-existent security.

But outside was worse. Everywhere I looked I saw destruction. Buildings pancaked on top of each other, roads cracked and uneven; basic utilities and infrastructure destroyed. Seven weeks after the region's most devastating natural disaster people still walked around in a daze, shell-shocked from the tragedy. Virtually everyone experienced the loss of loved ones. Many people narrowly escaped death themselves once buildings began to sway.

My journey to Haiti began months earlier. I watched initial news reports of an earthquake in the late afternoon on January 12th, 2010. Details proved elusive, but everything pointed to widespread destruction. Within 24 hours, the leadership at Antioch rallied to seek God, and immediately recognized we must respond.

But any response was complicated. The airport shut down entirely and the presidential palace collapsed, alongside hospitals and police stations. In fact, the scale of this crisis prevented effective government for several months. After three long days, our first medical teams crossed the border from the Dominican Republic and immediately spent the night treating intense trauma wounds at a woefully understaffed hospital. It was a scene reminiscent of a war zone. The next day, they ventured into the city and found an equally chaotic environment.

Back in Waco, we worked around the clock to scramble more medical teams. We gathered supplies, sought transportation, and nationally recruited trained specialists to work in makeshift clinics. Meanwhile, the team on the ground coordinated with the United Nations and countless agencies seeking to stem the suffering.

And so it was, weeks later, that I struggled into a dilapidated van. The hour-long ride provided me an unwelcome opportunity to reflect. My energy had been dominated for weeks by the logistical demands of setting up our transportation and supplies, and it wasn't until we bumped along the broken streets that the scale of human pain overwhelmed me.

What did we, a few foreigners, have to offer in the face of so much suffering? As we continued to struggle through to our destination, I began to question the point of our efforts. I knew we'd help people in need, but it felt like a drop in the bucket. I coveted the peace of my home, which felt like a galaxy away from the surrounding misery. It seemed easier to ignore the pain entirely.

This wasn't my first time to hit this wall. I felt it in Iraq in 2004 while listening to stories of chemical attacks and torture from my Kurdish friends. I saw it in Afghanistan a few years later as I witnessed the hardships native to three decades of non-stop violence and oppression. And I've felt it here in the States watching people struggle through the pain of broken marriages, addiction, chronic disease, and depression, only to name a few.

When faced with overpowering need, our natural response is often to do nothing at all. Rather than face the pain head on, we instead retreat to comfort. While we grieve for the suffering of others, our efforts seem insignificant, eventually deceiving us into believing the subtle message that if we cannot do *everything* then we cannot do *anything*. If we acquiesce, this messages grows into self-fulfilling prophesy.

This tension stands as a dangerous obstacle in the path of discipleship. Discipleship is transformative when everyone does his or her part; if we believe the lie that *my part* is irrelevant then it removes the very people critical to see lasting change. Discipleship is not contingent on a few powerful people doing everything, rather it works only when everyone does

> DISCIPLESHIP IS NOT CONTINGENT ON A FEW POWERFUL PEOPLE DOING EVERYTHING, RATHER IT WORKS ONLY WHEN EVERYONE DOES SOMETHING.

something. This hurdle is both universal and ancient. And Jesus demonstrated the solution.

2+5=5000

The biblical story of Jesus feeding the multitude vividly illustrates this tension, and the experience left a lasting impression on the disciples. It all began when Jesus was tired. He and the disciples ministered non-stop for days, and when they tried to rest by leaving town, thousands of people sought to join them. As Jesus gazed at the assembled multitude, He recognized their pain and their suffering. Despite His fatigue, He welcomed the interruption and taught the crowds.

It was a long day on the hillside until the disciples eventually determined people ought to return home for dinner, perhaps equally interested in getting a break themselves. But, in this weary moment, Jesus shocked His followers with an entirely unreasonable request: *You feed them.*

The disciples looked over the gathered thousands, completely unable to comprehend their Master's irrational demand. They appealed by citing the enormous cost required to just give each a bite. His request was simply impossible.

Jesus patiently listened but never responded to their appeal. Instead, He asked an entirely different question: "How much do you have?"

Five loaves and two fish was nothing compared to the hunger of this massive crowd. To consider it a solution was laughable. This amount was intended as a modest lunch for one person. To distribute to thousands essentially ensured everyone would receive a crumb, while the original owner would go hungry.

What could the disciples offer in the face of this immediate need? Sure, they could do something but it was just a drop in the bucket. They experienced the same tension we all confront. But despite their reluctance, they obeyed their Master's command.

Jesus lifted their sacrifice to Heaven, gave thanks, broke it, and handed it out to the surrounding throng. The disciples watched in amazement as their small offering multiplied to feed the masses. Jesus never asked His followers to gather enough food for everyone; instead, He asked them to give what they had – and He did the rest. The story proved the Messiah's supernatural power to the assembled multitude, but it also taught the disciples a powerful lesson: When faced with human need, God doesn't ask us to provide everything, but instead He asks us to give what we have and watch Him multiply it.

OUR ROLE

This passage illustrates the unique role of mankind within God's redemptive plan. Why did Jesus require the few loaves and fish for this miracle? In the Old Testament, He supernaturally provided Manna and meat to the Israelites in the desert. He fed a multitude far larger, and didn't need anyone's lunch to do so. What changed?

We need to review the basic story of the Bible to answer our question. Jesus died on the cross to pay the penalty for our sin. He rose from the dead to give us new life, and He filled us with His Spirit to restore us back to a full relationship with Him. Our spiritual rebirth reinstates us back to God's original plan as described in Genesis 1:28:

> God blessed them and said to them, "Be fruitful and increase in number; fill the earth and subdue it. Rule over the fish in the sea and the birds in the sky and over every living creature that moves on the ground."

God created Adam to live a life of spiritual blessing and close relationship with the Father. But He also called him to a life lived on mission. God commissioned Adam to fill the earth with His glory *before sin* robbed our inheritance. Part of His plan, before the creation of the world, was for us – you and me – to extend His Kingdom across the globe. Yes, sin warped God's design, but God took sin itself and wove it into His beautiful picture of grace. Our identity was redeemed and our calling restored.

Jesus fully intends to multiply His message to every tribe, tongue, language, and nation. And He fully intends to use us to do it. But to play our part, we need to give our few loaves and fish. We need to confront our insecurity and step out by faith into someone else's place of need. You cannot meet the needs of your city; you cannot even meet the needs of your Lifegroup. But you can give what you have: Invite a co-worker over for dinner, call a guest from church, initiate a discipleship group, and above all, keep showing up. Give your little and watch God multiply it to the masses. Remember Jason's story from the first chapter? One of the most pivotal moments in his transformation was a simple 'hello' in the church lobby.

The week in Haiti proved significant. We built a relationship with a small, forgotten community destroyed by the quake. The scale of destruction was vast, beyond any of our capacity to fix. Rather than retreat, we pressed in and gave the little we had, recognizing that the solution to the devastation in Haiti was the Haitians and a God who multiplies loaves and fish.

Several Antioch members moved to the region and immediately focused on developing Haitians as the central strategy. Our team sought to let the locals determine the plan and to evaluate the needs. We provided support as needed, but ultimately focused on our partners. Multiplying Godly Haitian leaders became the primary mission with a simple goal of finding one, who in turn developed a few more, who then continued the same with even more.

Eventually this led to physically rebuilding over a hundred homes, providing medical training and education support to multiple communities, and planting churches. Multiplication is limitless, as long as we each continue our part.

This is Haiti's hope. This is America's hope. And it's God's plan for the world.

OUR RESPONSE: MULTIPLY

Addition will never reach the world. No matter how gifted, a few superstar Christians simply cannot fulfill the Great Commission. The primary culprit is math. Imagine identifying the most gifted evangelist, logistics coordinator, fundraiser, and worship leader. We could release them to travel the globe to host Gospel crusades in order to finish the Mission. But even if they reached 300,000 people daily, we'd still fall behind global population growth. Then throw in cultural differences, language barriers, security problems, and learning styles – never mind the additional two billion people living today who haven't heard the Gospel. On top of it all, our charge is to *disciple* all the nations, not just *evangelize* them. The addition approach is hopeless.

Fortunately, God steers us down a different path. His plan relies on the faithful masses, not the gifted few. Let's consider the multiplication approach instead: One person disciples two, who then disciples two more, who then do the same. This continues, doubling every year. Within one generation, thirty-three years, the entire world can be *discipled*. No superstars needed.

Develop Everyone

Jesus charged us to *"obey all that I have commanded you,"* which includes the command to *"go and make disciples."* You cannot be a disciple unless you seek to also make a disciple. Every believer inherits the mission of God.

Respond by empowering each group member to discover the call of God on their life to disciple others. Help them identify where they are called to "go" by listing out five people they will reach out to. Discuss ways to live on mission – start with daily prayer, look for opportunities to serve, and discover creative ways to share a testimony.

Set this standard early in the life of the group. Often the most effective people are the most recent converts because they still maintain deep relational ties with other non-believers. These newly minted disciple-makers can share what they've received just a few weeks prior while you provide coaching. In other words, keep it multiplying.

As you disciple others and lead Lifegroup, view it as your primary mission to develop those in your groups. This includes training them to make disciples; it also includes empowering them to identify and grow their other spiritual gifts. Your goal is to work yourself out of a job.

God distributes a wide variety of spiritual gifts to the Church. Identifying and releasing these giftings empowers the Church to fulfill her Mission. However, if we fail to develop others then the entirety of ministry falls on a few people, overwhelming them and limiting the reproduction of the Church.

Many groups struggle to find leaders; this problem often originates from a flawed development perspective which waits to raise up people until they are needed. But by the time they are necessary, it's too late; the development process requires time.

Compare that approach to a discipleship perspective, which instead encourages developing people when they are ready, not when they are needed. If you disciple five people, each with a capacity to lead, then train all of them. Rather than develop one leader, release all five to start new groups and multiply the Kingdom!

This principle applies to every gifting: administration, worship, prophetic, teaching, and more. Help disciples identify their gifting, and then steer them toward training opportunities alongside mature believers. Look for chances for them to step out – leading worship in Lifegroup, organizing a group outreach, or volunteering in other areas in the church.

The process takes time, but eventually you'll wake up one day to discover a group filled with mature, gifted believers who are ready to multiply the Kingdom to the world around them.

Raise Up New Lifegroup Leaders

Identifying and developing new group leaders is critical to the health of a disciple-making church. Existing leaders serve on the front lines in this effort.

IDENTIFYING AND DEVELOPING NEW GROUP LEADERS IS CRITICAL TO THE HEALTH OF A DISCIPLE-MAKING CHURCH.

Every group should seek to actively develop new leaders through an intern process. Interns should exhibit the character qualities found in Chapter Two and demonstrate a desire to lead. Group leaders should inform the pastoral staff of their church prior to initiating with someone to intern.

Once an intern accepts, set a defined training period, generally for 1-2 months. Walk them through this book in its entirety and empower them to lead elements of the Lifegroup. Provide coaching prior and then give feedback after in order to maximize experiential learning.

MULTIPLY LIFEGROUPS

The goal to develop leaders must extend far beyond merely replacing existing leaders with new ones. We should instead seek to multiply leaders in order to launch new groups.

I recommend deploying two primary methods for creating new Lifegroups: *Multiplication* and *Planting*.

Multiplying

Multiplication describes a process by which a group grows to a large size and then splits into two, with one group led by the existing leader and the other by the new intern. In this scenario, leaders should communicate vision to the group for the upcoming change for at least two months prior, and then help guide the new group's formation based on existing relational ties.

The primary drawback to this process is the rupture of relational consistency; if groups multiply too quickly, then members may feel a relational disconnection.

Planting

Planting describes the process of sending out several people to start a new group from scratch while the majority of the existing group remains. The new group should define a clear vision and outreach strategy. I generally recommend at least two couples or three singles form the nucleus of the group before launching. At my church, we primarily use this approach to start new family Lifegroups.

Dying

All Lifegroups have a lifecycle, and it's not a bad thing. I've generally found groups start to die after three or four years, unless they relaunch with newly defined purpose. This process isn't inherently negative; in fact, it's often in this environment that people discover fresh vision to start something new.

If you find yourself leading a dying group, help it to die with dignity. Celebrate the wonderful things God has done in members' lives over the past several years. Encourage each member to seek the Lord for fresh purpose for next steps, even encouraging some to launch new groups of their own. Throughout the process, shepherd the group toward a new place of connection so that no one slips through the cracks.

This process isn't easy at first, but often leads to wonderful new ventures.

TIME FOR A PERSPECTIVE SHIFT

As we conclude, consider one last question: *Can you feed your city with an apple?*

Pause. Think about your answer.

The kneejerk response is to scoff at the ridiculous question. One little apple? Of course not! But if you reacted this way, you'd be wrong. The answer is *yes*.

You can feed a city with an apple, but only with a perspective change. Rather than seeing a solitary apple, you must instead see the seeds. Seeds grow to become trees; trees produce more apples, which in turn produce more seeds. The growth is limitless.

When we limit our perspective to just the apple, we try to cut and slice so that as many people as possible get a small bite. Ultimately, in the end everyone stays hungry. But if we change our view and refocus to instead plant the seeds, everyone ends up satisfied.

The Church needs a perspective shift. Rather than emphasizing a few big apples, let's instead focus on multiplying the seeds. Let's each disciple a few who in turn each disciple a few more; if we follow the example of Jesus there truly is no limit.

Stop for a moment and consider your legacy. Ten years from now, what impact will you have made? Think further, what about twenty years? Thirty? What will last once you are gone? Apple trees take a long time to grow, but once mature, will remain a long time. Discipleship is no different. We need fresh faith to embrace the Great

Commission and trust the example of Jesus instead of acquiescing to the slow current of a lifestyle dominated by the ever-present idol of the quick fix.

A raging fire ignites from a single spark and a massive tree begins as a lowly seed. You may feel inadequate; you may feel disqualified – just like every other person God has ever used. Welcome to the club. Despite your weaknesses, will you still resolve to live out the Great Commission? Will you 'Go Make Disciples'? If you do, I'm convinced you will witness lasting impact. And if we all do, then I'm convinced we will see our world transformed.

Discussion

Who can you ask to lead alongside of you?

What other giftings are present within the members of your group? How can you call them out?

If you are launching a new group, who will make up the nucleus of this new group? What will the first three or four weeks look like in order to establish the group?

Who can you encourage to launch a new group?

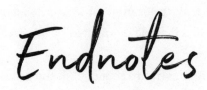

Endnotes

[1] Bewsher, Rick and Diane. *Tending Your Heart.* Find on The Antioch Discipleship App

[2] Anderson, Neil T. *The Steps to Freedom in Christ.* Bethany House Publishers, 2011.

[3] Hybels, Bill. *Courageous Leadership.* Zondervan, 2009.

Contact

FACEBOOK: DREW STEADMAN

INSTAGRAM: @DREWSTEADMAN

TWITTER: @DREWSTEADMAN1

WEBSITE: ANTIOCHCC.COM

Notes

e **Antioch Discipleship App** is designed to help you love God, love others and reach out. It will equip
u to disciple others and help them grow in their relationship with Jesus, while helping you do the
me. It can easily be used in a group setting, one-on-one or in your own personal devotional time.

e Antioch Discipleship App is for anyone who...

Wants to learn about God

Is new to faith

Wants to know more about Kingdom values

It includes....

- Bible reading

- Questions to help you study and understand Scripture

- Action steps to help you apply what you learn

FOREWORD BY **MAX LUCADO**

PASSION & PURPOSE

BELIEVING THE CHURCH CAN STILL CHANGE THE WORLD

JIMMY SEIBERT